D0984994

READINGS IN THE
HISTORY OF EDUCATION

AMS PRESS
NEW YORK

READINGS IN THE HISTORY OF EDUCATION

MEDIAEVAL UNIVERSITIES

By ARTHUR O. NORTON

*Assistant Professor of the History and Art of Teaching
in Harvard University*

CAMBRIDGE

PUBLISHED BY HARVARD UNIVERSITY

1909

Reprinted from the edition of 1909, Cambridge, Mass.
First AMS EDITION published 1971
Manufactured in the United States of America

International Standard Book Number: 0-404-04797-1

Library of Congress Catalog Number: 78-173801

AMS PRESS INC.
NEW YORK, N.Y.

PREFACE

THESE readings in the history of mediaeval universities
are the first installment of a series, which I have planned
with the view of illustrating, mainly from the sources,
the history of modern education in Europe and America.
They are intended for use after the manner of the source
books or collections of documents which have so vastly
improved the teaching of general history in recent years.
No argument is needed as to the importance of such a
collection for effective teaching of the history of education; but I would urge that the subject requires in a
peculiar degree rich and full illustration from the sources.
The life of school, college, or university is varied, vivid,
even dramatic, while we live it; but, once it has passed,
it becomes thinner and more spectral than almost any
other historical fact. Its original records are, in all con-
science, thin enough; the situation is still worse when
they are worked over at third or fourth hand, flattened
out, smoothed down, and desiccated in the pages of a
modern history of education. Such histories are of
course necessary to effective teaching of the subject;
but the records alone can clothe the dry bones of fact
with flesh and blood. Only by turning back to them
do we gain a sense of personal intimacy with the past;
only thus can we realize that schools and universities
of other days were not less real than those of to-day,

teachers and students of other generations not less vividly alive than we, academic questions not less unsettled or less eagerly debated. To gain this sense of concrete, living reality in the history of education is one of the most important steps toward understanding the subject.

In selecting and arranging the records here presented I have had in mind chiefly the needs of students who are taking the usual introductory courses in the subject. Students of general history — a subject in which more and more account is taken of culture in the broad sense of the term — may also find them useful.

Within the necessarily limited space I have chosen to illustrate in some detail a few aspects of the history of mediaeval universities rather than to deal briefly with a large number of topics. Many important matters, not here touched upon, are reserved for future treatment. Some documents pertinent to the topics here discussed are not reproduced because they are easily accessible elsewhere; these are mentioned in the bibliographical note at the close of the volume.

In writing the descriptive and explanatory text I have attempted only to indicate the general significance of the translations, and to supply information not easily obtained, or not clearly given in the references or textbooks which, it is assumed, the student will read in connection with this work. It would be possible to write a commentary of genuinely mediaeval proportions on the selections here given; doubtless many of the details would be clearer for such a commentary. Some of these are explained by cross-references in the body of the text; in the main, however, I have preferred to let the documents stand for their face value to the average reader.

I have given especial attention to university studies
(pp. 37–80) and university exercises (pp. 107–134) because these important subjects are unusually difficult for
most students, and because surprisingly few illustrations
of them from the sources have been heretofore easily
accessible in English. In particular, there has not been,
I believe, a previous translation of any considerable
passage from the much discussed and much criticised
mediaeval commentaries on university text-books. The
selection here given (pp. 59–75) is not intended for
continuous reading; but it will fully repay close and
repeated examination. Not infrequently single sentences
of this commentary are the outcroppings of whole volumes of mediaeval thought and controversy; indeed
anyone who follows to the end each of the lines of study
suggested will have at command a very respectable bit
of knowledge concerning the intellectual life of the
middle ages. The passage requires more explanation
by the teacher, or more preliminary knowledge on the
part of the student, than any other selection in the book.

The sources from which the selections have been made
are indicated in the footnotes to the text. My great
indebtedness to Mr. Hastings Rashdall's "Universities
of Europe in the Middle Ages" is also there indicated.
Messrs. G. P. Putnam's Sons and Mr. Joseph McCabe
generously gave me permission to quote more extensive
passages from the latter's brilliant biography of Abelard
than I finally found it possible to use. Mr. Charles S.
Moore has been my chief assistant in the preparation
of the manuscript; most of the translations not otherwise credited are due to his careful work, but I am
responsible for the version finally adopted in numerous
passages in which the interpretation depends on a knowl-

edge of detailed historical facts. In conclusion, I have to thank Professor Charles H. Haskins and Professor Leo Wiener for information which has spared me many days of research on obscure details, and Professor Paul H. Hanus for suggestions which have contributed to the clearness of the text.

A. O. N.

CONTENTS

READINGS IN THE HISTORY OF EDUCATION

I

INTRODUCTION

THE history of education, like all other branches of history, is based upon documents. Historical documents are, in general, " the traces which have been left by the thoughts and actions of men of former times "; the term commonly refers to the original records or *sources* from which our knowledge of historical facts is derived. The documents most generally used by historians are written or printed. In the history of education alone these are of the greatest variety; as is shown in the following pages, among them are university charters, proceedings, regulations, lectures, text-books, the statutes of student organizations, personal letters, autobiographies, contemporary accounts of university life, and laws made by civil or ecclesiastical authorities to regulate university affairs. Similar varieties of records exist for other educational institutions and activities. The immense masses of such written or printed materials produced to-day, even to the copy-book of the primary school and the student's note-book of college lectures, will, if they survive, become documents for the future historian of education.

The known sources for the history of education in western Europe since the twelfth century — to go no further afield — are exceedingly numerous, and widely spread among various public and private collections; the labor of a lifetime would hardly suffice to examine them all critically. Nevertheless many printed and written documents have been collected, edited, and published in their original languages; and in some instances the collections are fairly complete, or at least fairly representative of the documents in existence. Assuming that they are accurate copies of the original records, many are now easily accessible to students of the subject, since these reproductions may be owned by all large libraries.

These records, rightly apprehended, have far more than a mere antiquarian interest. The history of mediaeval universities is profoundly important, not only for students, but also for administrators, of modern higher education. For to a surprising degree the daily and hourly conduct of university affairs of the twentieth century is influenced by what universities did six centuries ago. On this point the words of Mr. Hastings Rashdall, a leading authority on mediaeval universities, are instructive: " . . . If we would completely understand the meaning of offices, titles, ceremonies, organizations preserved in the most modern, most practical, most unpicturesque of the institutions which now bear the name of ' University,' we must go back to the earliest days of the earliest Universities that ever existed, and trace the history of their chief successors through the seven centuries that intervene between the rise of Bologna or Paris, and the foundation of the new University of Strassburg in Germany, or of the Victoria University in England."

Knowledge of the subject should, however, yield much more than understanding: it should also influence the practical attitudes of those who are concerned with university affairs. Here I take issue with those historians who hold that history supplies no " information of practical utility in the conduct of life "; no " lessons directly profitable to individuals and peoples." The evidence cannot be exhibited here, but such information notoriously has been of the utmost practical value in education, both in shaping influential theories and in determining even minute details of educational practice. There is no reason to suppose that it may not continue to be thus serviceable. Other utilities of university history are less direct, but not less important. The study of individual institutions and their varying circumstances and problems " prepares us to understand and tolerate a variety of usages "; the study of their growth not only " cures us of a morbid dread of change," but also leads us to view their progressive adaptation to new conditions as necessary and desirable. If such study teaches only these two lessons to those who may hereafter shape the course of educational affairs it more than justifies itself. For to eradicate that intolerance of variety in educational practice so characteristic of the academic man of the past, and to diminish in future generations his equally characteristic opposition to changes involving adaptation to new conditions, is to render one of the greatest possible services to educational progress.

THE RENAISSANCE OF THE TWELFTH CENTURY

DURING the twelfth century a great educational revival manifested itself in western Europe, following upon several centuries of intellectual decline or relative inactivity. Though its beginnings may be traced into the eleventh century, and though its culmination belongs to a much later period, the movement is often called the Renaissance of the Twelfth Century. In that century it first appears as a widely diffused and rapidly growing movement, and it then takes on distinctly the characteristics which mark its later development. The revival appears first in Italy and France; from these regions it spreads during the next three centuries into England, Spain, Germany, Denmark, Sweden, and Scotland.

Certain facts concerning this educational Renaissance should be clearly understood in connection with the following selections:

1. To men of the times it first showed itself as a renewal of activity in existing schools. Here and there appeared eminent teachers ; to them resorted increasing numbers of students from greater and greater distances. In a few years some of these institutions became schools of international fame. The newly roused enthusiasm for study in France at the opening of the twelfth century is thus described by a modern writer:

The scholastic fever, which was soon to inflame the youth of the whole of Europe, had already set in. You could not travel far over the rough roads of France without meeting some footsore scholar, making for the nearest large monastery or cathedral town. Before many years, it is true, there arose an elaborate system of conveyance from town to town, an organization of messengers to run between the chateau and the school ; but in the earlier days, and, to some extent, even later, the scholar wandered afoot through the long provinces of France. Robbers, frequently in the service of the lord of the land, infested every province. It was safest to don the coarse frieze tunic of the pilgrim, without pockets, sling your little wax tablets and stylus at your girdle, strap a wallet of bread and herbs and salt on your back, and laugh at the nervous folk who peeped out from their coaches over a hedge of pikes and daggers. Few monasteries refused a meal or a rough bed to the wandering scholar. Rarely was any fee exacted for the lesson given. For the rest, none were too proud to earn a few sous by sweeping, or drawing water, or amusing with a tune on the reed-flute ; or to wear the cast-off tunics of their masters.[1]

This account refers to the study of logic and theology, which soon became dominant in Paris and in various cathedral schools in other parts of France. With slight modifications it would describe also the revival of interest in Roman law in Italy, especially at Bologna.

2. The revival was concerned mainly with professional, or — as later appeared — university, education. The prevailing interest was in Law, Medicine, Theology, and the philosophy of Aristotle. Schools of lower grade were much influenced by the intellectual activity of the times, but the characteristic product of this movement was the university. The universities, organized as cor-

[1] Adapted from Joseph McCabe, *Abelard*, pp. 7, 8.

porations, with their teachers divided into faculties, their definite courses of study, their examinations, their degrees, their privileges, and their cosmopolitan communities of students, were not only the result of the revival, but they were institutions essentially new in the history of education, and the models for all universities which have since been established.

3. Between the latter part of the twelfth century and 1500 A. D. at least seventy-nine universities were established in western Europe. There may have been others of which no trace remains. Several of them were shortlived, some lasting but a few years; ten disappeared before 1500. Since that date twenty others have become extinct. The forty-nine European universities of to-day which were founded before 1500 have all passed through many changes in character and various periods of prosperity and decline, but we still recognize in them the characteristic features mentioned above, and the same features reappear in the "most modern, most practical, most unpicturesque of the institutions which now bear the name of 'University.'" This is one illustration of the statement on page 2 that the daily and hourly conduct of university affairs in the twentieth century is to a suprising degree influenced by what universities did seven centuries ago.

4. The term "University" has always been difficult to define. In the Middle Ages its meaning varied in different places, and changed somewhat in the centuries between 1200 and 1500 A. D. In these pages it signifies in general an institution for higher education; and "institution" means, not a group of buildings, but a so-

ciety of teachers or students organized, and ultimately incorporated, for mutual aid and protection, and for the purpose of imparting or securing higher education. Originally, universities were merely guilds of Masters or Scholars; as such they were imitations of the numerous guilds of artisans and tradesmen already in existence. Out of the simple organization and customs of these guilds grew the elaborate organization and ceremonials of later universities.

There were two main types of university organization,— the University of Masters, and the University of Students. In the former, — which is the type of all modern universities, — the government and instruction of students were regulated by the Masters or Doctors. In the latter, these matters were controlled by the students, who also prescribed rules for the conduct of the Masters. Paris and Bologna were, respectively, the original representatives of these types. Paris was the original University of Masters; its pattern was copied, with some modifications, by the universities of England, Germany, Denmark, Sweden, and Scotland. Bologna was the archetypal University of Students; its organization was imitated, also with variations, by the universities of Italy, France (except Paris), Spain, and Portugal.

In and after the thirteenth century, the place or school in which a university existed was almost always called a *Studium Generale*, i. e. a place to which students resorted, or were invited, from all countries. This term was used in contrast to *Studium Particulare*, i.e. any school in which a Master in a town taught a few schol-

In the *Studium Generale* instruction was given by

several Masters, in one or more of the Faculties of Arts, Law, Medicine, and Theology. In time the term came to be synonymous with "University"; it is so used in this book.

5. The theoretically complete mediaeval university contained the four faculties of Arts, Theology, Law, and Medicine. These we find reproduced in some modern universities. Then, as now, however, it was not common to find them all equally well developed in any single institution; many possessed only two or three faculties, and some had but one. There are rare instances of five faculties, owing to the subdivision of Law. At Paris, the strongest faculties were those of Arts and Theology; Law and Medicine were in comparison but feebly represented. At Bologna, on the other hand, the study of Law was predominant, although the Arts, Medicine, and Theology were also taught there.

6. The studies pursued in the various faculties in and after the thirteenth century were in general as follows:

In the Faculty of Arts:

1. The "three philosophies" — Natural, Moral, and Rational — of Aristotle, together with his Logic, Rhetoric, and Politics. Of these, Logic and Rhetoric are included below.

2. The Seven Liberal Arts, comprising

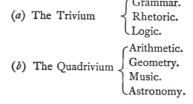

(*a*) The Trivium { Grammar. Rhetoric. Logic.

(*b*) The Quadrivium { Arithmetic. Geometry. Music. Astronomy.

In the Faculty of Law:

1. The *Corpus Juris Civilis*, or body of Roman Civil Law, compiled at Constantinople 529–533 A. D., under direction of the Roman Emperor Justinian.

2. The Canon Law, or law governing the Church, of which the first part was compiled by the monk Gratian about the year 1142. His compilation of the Canon Law is usually referred to as the *Decretum Gratiani.*

In the Faculty of Theology:

1. The " Sentences " of Peter Lombard.
2. The Bible.

In the Faculty of Medicine:

1. The works of Hippocrates.
2. The works of Galen.
3. Medical treatises of various Arabic and Jewish writers of the seventh century A. D. and later.

These studies will be described more fully in connection with the selections on pages 37–83.

Not all of the works mentioned under these divisions were included in the regular programme of any university; the actual studies required for the various degrees consisted rather in selections from these works. The selections chosen varied somewhat in different universities; moreover, the course in any given university changed from time to time. Consequently the degrees of A. B. and A. M., as well as degrees in Law, Medicine, and Theology, probably never represented exactly the same set of studies in any considerable number of universities, nor did they even represent exactly the same work for many years in any single university. This corresponds exactly with the situation in modern universities, although at present the variations in studies for the same degree are greater and the changes in any given university are usually more rapid than they were in the universities of the Middle Ages.

It is necessary to remember that all the text-books were in Latin. Those written originally in other tongues were translated into Latin. All university exercises were conducted in that language, and frequently the regulations required students to use Latin in conversation outside the lecture halls. Latin was, in short, the universal academic tongue. Obviously, the use of the same language everywhere facilitated the migration of students and teachers from one university to another.

7. Although the first universities were not established as organized institutions until the latter part of the twelfth century, the intellectual movement which gave rise to them was well under way a century earlier. It showed itself first in the rise of great teachers, some of whom were also notable scholars. There has never been a clearer demonstration of the central importance in education of the distinguished teacher:

At the beginning of the twelfth century three schools are distinguished in the contemporary literature above the multitude which had sprung into new life in France and were connected with so many of her cathedrals and religious houses. These three were at Laon, Paris, and Chartres. It would be more accurate to say, they were the schools of Anselm and Ralph, of William of Champeaux, and of Bernard Sylvester. For in those days the school followed the teacher, not the teacher the school. Wherever a master lived, there he taught; and thither, in proportion to his renown, students assembled from whatever quarter. . . . The tie was a personal one, and was generally severed by the master's death. A succession of great teachers in one place was a rare exception; nor is such an exception afforded by the history of any of the three schools to which we have referred.[1]

In these days, when education requires a more and more elaborate equipment of buildings, libraries, laboratories, and museums, it is no longer possible for teachers, however distinguished, to attract throngs of students to places absolutely unprovided with the resources for teaching, or to provide these resources anywhere on the spur of the moment. In the twelfth century, on the contrary, the only necessary equipment consisted in the master, his small library which could be carried by one man; wax tablets, or pens, ink, and vellum or parchment for the students; and any kind of a shelter which would serve as a protection from the weather. Not even benches or chairs were necessary, for students commonly sat upon the straw-strewn floors of the lecture rooms. Thus the school might easily follow the teacher in his migrations, and easily sink into obscurity or disappear upon his death or cessation from teaching. The autobiography of Abelard (see page 14), recounts an experience unusual in itself, but perfectly illustrative of the point. After relating various misfortunes and persecutions he continues:

So I betook myself to a certain wilderness previously known to me, and there on land given to me by certain ones, with the consent of the Bishop of the region, I constructed out of reeds

[1] R. L. Poole, *Illustrations from the History of Medieval Thought*, p. 109.

and straw a sort of oratory in the name of the Holy Trinity where, in company with one of our clergy, I might truly chan to the Lord : "Lo I have wandered far off, and have remainec in the wilderness."

As soon as Scholars learned this they began to gather from every side, leaving cities and castles to dwell in the wilderness. and in place of their spacious homes to build small tabernacles for themselves, and in place of delicate food to live on herbs of the fields and coarse bread, and in place of soft couches to make up [beds of] straw and grass, and in place of tables to pile up sods.[1]

[1] *Petri Abaelardi Opera*, edd. Cousin et Jourdain, I, p. 25.

III

THE RISE OF MEDIAEVAL UNIVERSITIES

THE influences contributing to the rise of universities were numerous, and in many cases obscure. The most important were: 1. Inspiring and original teachers, who gathered about them great numbers of students. 2. A new method of teaching. 3. A new group of studies. 4. Privileges granted to scholars and masters by civil and ecclesiastical authorities. 5. The direct initiative of those authorities in establishing universities by decree. The readings which follow are chosen to illustrate these influences.

1. TEACHERS AND STUDENTS OF THE TWELFTH CENTURY

(a) *A Pre-University Teacher: Abelard*

Among the teachers of the early part of the twelfth century, two were of especial significance in the later intellectual development of the period, — Irnerius (*ca.* 1070–1130) at Bologna, and Abelard (1079–1142) at Paris. They were the forerunners of the universities which began to take form at the end of the twelfth century in those cities. Irnerius marks a new epoch in the study of the body of Roman Law; following the traditions of teaching which he established, the University of

Bologna became the most prominent school of law in Europe. In a similar way Abelard marks at Paris the introduction of a new method of teaching and investigation, an attitude of intellectual independence on theological questions, and a permanently influential position in scholastic philosophy; following his initiative the University of Paris became the leading school of Philosophy and Theology. These two institutions — Bologna and Paris — were in turn the models for all other mediaeval universities, not only in organization, but also so far as the study of Law, Theology, and Philosophy was concerned. Hence, indirectly, the influence of Abelard and Irnerius was widely diffused and long continued.

The documents relating to Irnerius are scanty. For a discussion of his influence on the teaching of Roman Law, see Rashdall, I, ch. iv, and especially pages 121–127. Concerning Abelard the records are abundant.

Abelard, the eldest son of a noble family of Pallet (Palais), Brittany, was in his day the most renowned teacher in France. Instead of becoming the head of his family and adopting the career of a soldier, he abandoned his birthright and the profession of arms for the life of the scholar and the battlefields of debate. His early life as a student wandering from school to school is thus described by himself:

The more fully and easily I advanced in the study of letters the more ardently I clung to them, and I became so enamored of them that, abandoning to my brothers the pomp of glory, together with my inheritance and the rights of the eldest son, I resigned from the Councils of War that I might

be educated in the camp of Minerva. And since among all
the weapons of philosophy I preferred the arms of logic, I ex-
changed accoutrements and preferred the conflicts of debate to
the trophies of war. Thenceforward I walked through the
various provinces engaging in debates wherever I had heard
that the study of this art [logic] flourished, and thus became a
rival of the Peripatetics.

At length [about 1100 A. D.] I reached Paris, where for
some time this art had been prospering, and went to William
of Champeaux, my instructor, distinguished at the time in this
particular by his work and reputation as a teacher. Staying
with him for a while, I was at first acceptable, but shortly after
was very annoying to him, namely, when I tried to refute some of
his opinions, and often ventured to argue against him and, not
seldom, seemed to surpass him in debate.[1]

In scholis militare — to wage war in the schools —
was the phrase aptly used to describe this mode of
debate. William of Champeaux was then the head of
the cathedral school of Notre Dame and the leading
teacher of logic in France. " Within a few months
Abelard made his authority totter, and set his reputation on the wane. In six or seven years he drove him
in shame and humiliation from his chair, after a contest
which filled Christendom with its echoes." By overcoming William in debate he established his own reputation as a teacher. At various times between 1108
and 1139 he taught in Paris, whither crowds of students
came to hear him. His fame was at its height about
1117, shortly after his appointment to the chair which
William himself had held. Few teachers have ever
attracted a following so large and so devoted. His

[1] *History of my Calamities, l. c.* p. 4.

remarkable success in drawing to Paris students from all quarters is vividly described by a modern writer:

The pupil who had left Paris when both William and Abelard disappeared in 1113 would find a marvellous change on returning to it about 1116 or 1117. He would find the lecture hall and the cloister and the quadrangle, under the shadow of the great cathedral, filled with as motley a crowd of youths and men as any scene in France could show. Little groups of French and Norman and Breton nobles chattered together in their bright silks and fur-tipped mantles, with slender swords dangling from embroidered belts, vying with each other in the length and crookedness of their turned-up shoes. Anglo-Saxons looked on, in long fur-lined cloaks, tight breeches, and leathern hose swathed with bands of many colored cloth. Stern-faced northerners, Poles and Germans, in fur caps and with colored girdles and clumsy shoes, or with feet roughly tied up in the bark of trees, waited impatiently for the announcement of *Li Mestre*. Pale-faced southerners had braved the Alps and the Pyrenees under the fascination of "the wizard." Shaven and sandalled monks, black-habited clerics, black canons, secular and regular, black in face too, some of them, heresy hunters from the neighboring abbey of St. Victor, mingled with the crowd of young and old, grave and gay, beggars and nobles, sleek citizens and bronzed peasants. . . .

Over mountains and over seas the mingled reputation of the city and the school were carried, and a remarkable stream set in from Germany, Switzerland, Italy (even from proud Rome), Spain, and England ; even " distant Brittany sent you its animals to be instructed," wrote Prior Fulques to Abelard (a Breton) a year or two afterwards.[1]

What was there in the teaching of Abelard which brought together this extraordinary gathering? One

[1] McCabe, *Abelard*, pp. 75, 76, 78.

may admit the presence of unanalyzable genius in this master, and still find certain qualities indispensable to the efficient teacher of to-day, — a winning personality, fulness of knowledge, and technical skill as a teacher. These are admirably set forth in the following description:

It is not difficult to understand the charm of Abelard's teaching. Three qualities are assigned to it by the writers of the period, some of whom studied at his feet; clearness, richness in imagery, and lightness of touch are said to have been the chief characteristics of his teaching. Clearness is, indeed, a quality of his written works, though they do not naturally convey an impression of his oral power. His splendid gifts and versatility, supported by a rich voice, a charming personality, a ready and sympathetic use of human literature, and a freedom from excessive piety, gave him an immeasurable advantage over all the teachers of the day. Beside most of them, he was as a butterfly to an elephant. A most industrious study of the few works of Aristotle and of the Roman classics that were available, a retentive memory, an ease in manipulating his knowledge, a clear, penetrating mind, with a corresponding clearness of expression, a ready and productive fancy, a great knowledge of men, a warmer interest in things human than in things divine, a laughing contempt for authority, a handsome presence, and a musical delivery — these were his gifts.[1]

He takes his place in history, apart from the ever-interesting drama and the deep pathos of his life, in virtue of two distinctions. They are, firstly, an extraordinary ability in imparting such knowledge as the poverty of the age afforded — the facts of his career reveal it; and, secondly, a mind of such marvellous penetration that it conceived great truths which it has taken humanity seven or eight centuries to see — this will appear as we proceed. It was the former of these gifts that made him,

[1] *l. c.* p. 82.

2

in literal truth, the centre of learned and learning Christendom, the idol of several thousand eager scholars. Nor, finally, were these thousands the "horde of barbarians" that jealous Master Roscelin called them. It has been estimated that a pope, nineteen cardinals, and more than fifty bishops and archbishops were at one time among his pupils.[1]

Abelard's fame as a teacher, with the consequent increase of masters and students at Paris, undoubtedly paved the way for the formation of the University later in the century. This is not however his greatest distinction in the history of education. His most enduring influences came from (1) his independence in thinking, (2) his novel method of dealing with debatable questions, and (3) his contributions to scholastic philosophy and theology. The first two of these are considered below; the last belongs more properly to the history of philosophy.

(1) Nothing singles Abelard out more clearly among the teachers of his time than his intellectual independence. Most of his contemporaries accepted unquestioningly the view that in religious matters faith precedes reason. One might seek to justify one's faith by reason, but preliminary doubt as to what should be the specific articles of one's faith was inadmissible. As they supposed, these articles had been determined by the church fathers — Augustine, Jerome, and others — and by the Bible. Their view had been formulated by Anselm of Canterbury in the preceding century:

"I do not seek to know in order that I may believe, but I believe in order that I may know." "The Christian ought to

[1] *l. c.* p. 89.

advance to knowledge through faith, not come to faith through knowledge." "The proper order demands that we believe the deep things of Christian faith before we presume to reason about them."

With his keenly critical, questioning mind Abelard found a flaw in this position: on many questions of faith the authorities themselves disagreed. "In such cases," — he said in effect, — "how shall I come to any definite belief unless I first reason it out?" "By doubting we are led to inquiry, and by inquiry we attain the truth." His attitude — as contrasted with that of Anselm, given above — is set forth in the prologue to his *Sic et Non* (Yes and No):

In truth, constant or frequent questioning is the first key to wisdom; and it is, indeed, to the acquiring of this [habit of] questioning with absorbing eagerness that the famous philosopher, Aristotle, the most clear sighted of all, urges the studious when he says: "It is perhaps difficult to speak confidently in matters of this sort unless they have often been investigated. Indeed, to doubt in special cases will not be without advantage." For through doubting we come to inquiry and through inquiry we perceive the truth. As the Truth Himself says: "Seek and ye shall find, knock and it shall be opened unto you." And He also, instructing us by His own example, about the twelfth year of His life wished to be found sitting in the midst of the doctors, asking them questions, exhibiting to us by His asking of questions the appearance of a pupil, rather than, by preaching, that of a teacher, although there is in Him, nevertheless, the full and perfect wisdom of God.

Now when a number of quotations from [various] writings are introduced they spur on the reader and allure him into seeking the truth in proportion as the authority of the writing itself is commended. . . .

In accordance, then, with these forecasts it is our pleasure to collect different sayings of the holy Fathers as we planned, just as they have come to mind, suggesting (as they do) some questioning from their apparent disagreement, in order that they may stimulate tender readers to the utmost effort in seeking the truth and may make them keener as the result of their seeking.[1]

(2) The new method which Abelard formed for discovering the truth is presented in the " Yes and No." He first stated in the form of a thesis for debate the question on which doubt existed. The book contains one hundred and fifty-eight such questions. He then brought together under each question the conflicting opinions of various authorities, and, without stating his own view, left the student to reason for himself in the matter. There is no doubt that this method served his purpose to " stimulate tender readers to the utmost effort in seeking the truth." His boldness in considering some of these questions debatable at all, the novelty of the doubt which they imply, and their incisive challenge to keen thinking are evident from the following list :

1. That faith is based upon reason, *et contra.*
5. That God is not single, *et contra.*
6. That God is tripartite, *et contra.*
8. That in the Trinity it is not to be stated that there is more than one Eternal being, *et contra.*
11. That the Divine Persons mutually differ, *et contra.*
12. That in the Trinity each is one with the other, *et contra.*
13. That God the Father is the cause of the son, *et contra.*
14. That the Son is without beginning, *et contra.*
27. That God judges with foreknowledge, *et non.*

[1] *Ouvrages Inédits d'Abélard*, ed. V. Cousin, p. 16.

28. That the providence of God is the cause of things happening, *et non*.

32. That to God all things are possible, *et non*.

36. That God does whatever he wishes, *et non*.

37. That nothing happens contrary to the will of God, *et contra*.

38. That God knows all things, *et non*.

53. That Adam's sin was great, *et non*.

84. That man's first sin did not begin through the persuasion of the devil, *et contra*.

55. That Eve only, not Adam, was beguiled, *et contra*.

56. That by sinning man lost free will, *et non*.

69. That the Son of God was predestinated, *et contra*.

79. That Christ was a deceiver, *et non*.

85. That the hour of the Lord's resurrection is uncertain, *et contra*.

116. That the sins of the fathers are visited upon the children, *et contra*.

122. That everybody should be allowed to marry, *et contra*.

141. That works of sanctity do not justify a man, *et contra*.

144. That at times we all sin against our will, *et contra*.

150. That sins are not remitted without confession, *et contra*.

153. That a lie is never permissible, *et contra*.

154. That a man may destroy himself for some reasons, *et contra*.

155. That Christians may not for any reason kill a man, *et contra*.

156. That it is lawful to kill a man, *et non*.

How he brought out the conflict of opinions is shown by the following example:

THAT IT IS LAWFUL TO KILL A MAN, AND THE OPPOSITE THESIS.

Jerome on Isaiah, *Bk. V.* He who cuts the throat of a man of blood, is not a man of blood.

Idem, On the Epistle to the Galatians : He who smites the wicked because they are wicked and whose reason for the murder is that he may slay the base, is a servant of the Lord.

Idem, on Jeremiah : For the punishment of homicides, impious persons and poisoners is not bloodshed, but serving the law.

Cyprian, in the Ninth Kind of Abuse : The King ought to restrain theft, punish deeds of adultery, cause the wicked to perish from off the face of the earth, refuse to allow parricides and perjurers to live.

Augustine : Although it is manslaughter to slaughter a man, a person may sometimes be slain without sin. For both a soldier in the case of an enemy and a judge or his official in the case of a criminal, and the man from whose hand, perhaps without his will or knowledge, a weapon has flown, do not seem to me to sin, but merely to kill a man.

Likewise : The soldier is ordered by law to kill the enemy, and if he shall prove to have refrained from such slaughter, he pays the penalty at the hands of his commander. Shall we not go so far as to call these laws unjust or rather no laws at all? For that which was not just does not seem to me to be a law.

Idem, on Exodus ch. xxvii : The Israelites committed no theft in spoiling the Egyptians, but rendered a service to God at his bidding, just as when the servant of a judge kills a man whom the law hath ordered to be killed ; certainly if he does it of his own volition he is a homicide, even though he knows that the man whom he executes ought to be executed by the judge.

Idem, on Leviticus ch. lxxv : When a man is justly put to death, the law puts him to death, not thou.

Idem, Bk. I of the " City of God " : Thou shalt not kill, except in the case of those whose death God orders, or else when a law hath been passed to suit the needs of the time and express command hath been laid upon a person. But he does not kill who owes service to the person who gives him his orders, for he is as it were a mere sword for the person who employs his assistance.

Likewise: When a soldier, in obedience to the power under which he is legitimately placed, kills a man, by no law of the state is he accused of murder; nay if he has not done it, he is accused of desertion and insubordination. But if he had acted under his own initiative and of his own will, he would have incurred the charge of shedding human blood. And so he is punished if he does not do when ordered that for which he would receive punishment if he did it without orders.

Idem, to Publicola: Counsel concerning the slaying of men pleaseth me not, that none may be slain by them, unless perhaps a man is a soldier or in a public office, so that he does the deed not in his own behalf, but for others and for the state, accepting power legitimately conferred, if it is consonant with the task imposed on him.

Likewise: It has been said: let us not resist the evil man, let not the vengeance delight us which feeds the mind on others' ill, let us not neglect the reproofs of men.

Idem, to Marcella: If that earthly commonwealth of thine keep to the teachings of Christ, even wars will not be waged without goodwill, for with pitying heart even wars if possible will be waged by the good, so that the lusts of desire may be subdued and those faults destroyed which ought under just rule to be either rooted out or chastised. For if Christian training condemned all wars, this should rather be the advice given in the gospel for their safety to the soldiers who ask for it, namely to throw aside their arms and retire altogether from the field. But this is the word spoken to them: Do violence to no man, neither accuse any falsely; and be content with your wages.

He warns them that the wages that belong to them should satisfy them, but he by no means forbids them to take the field.

Idem, to his comrade Boniface: "I will give thee and thine a useful counsel: Take arms in thy hands; let prayer strike the ears of the creator; because in battle the heavens are opened, God looks forth and awards the victory to the side he sees to be the righteous one.

Idem : The wars to be waged we undertake either at the command of God or under some lawful rule. Else John when the soldiers to be baptized came to him saying, " And what shall we do?" would make answer to them : " Cast aside your arms, leave the service ; smite no man ; ruin no man."

But because he knew that they did these things because they were in the service, that they were not slayers of men, but servants of the law ; and not avengers of their own injuries, but guardians of the public safety, his answer to them was : " Do violence to no man," etc.

Isidore, Etymologiae, Bk. XVIII, ch. iii : A righteous war is one waged according to orders, to recover property or drive back the enemy.

Pope Nicholas to the questions of the Bulgarians : If there is no urgent need, not only in Lent but at all times, men should abstain from battles. If however there is an unavoidable and urgent occasion, and it is not Lent, beyond all doubt preparations for wars should be sparingly made in one's own defence or in that of one's country or the laws of one's fathers; lest forsooth this word be said : A man if he has an attack to make, does not carefully take counsel beforehand for his own safety and that of others, nor does he guard against injury to holy religion.[1]

This example shows the scholastic method in its earliest form, — the statement of the thesis, followed by the simple citation of authorities, *pro* and *con.* Later writers added the conclusion which they wished to support, or at least indicated it in the statement of the thesis. This, of course, robbed the method of much of its stimulus to independent thinking. Other modifi-

[1] *Sic et Non,* CLVI. The Latin text of this book is printed in *Ouvrages Inédits d'Abélard,* ed. V. Cousin.

cations also appeared. See the examples on pages 58 ff., 121 ff. The point to be noted here is that in the " Yes and No " Abelard struck out definitely the method which was followed for centuries in a large part of university instruction. How great a part it played can be understood only by an extended study of university history. A brief discussion of the subject is given on pages 35–37. The stimulating way in which Abelard used it was potent in drawing students to Paris. Among those who came to hear him was John of Salisbury.

(b) *A Pre-University Scholar: John of Salisbury*

John of Salisbury (c. 1120–1180), " for thirty years the central figure of English learning," " beyond dispute the best-read man of his time," is a good example of the more serious students among those who travelled abroad for study in the early days of the revival described above. He spent twelve years (1136–1148) at Paris and at Chartres. His " Metalogicus " (completed about 1159) is perhaps the best contemporary account of educational affairs in France in the twelfth century.

The book is interesting now mainly for its account of the writer's training, for its advocacy of liberal studies as a preparation for logic, and for its vigorous argument in favor of using all of the works of Aristotle then known, several of which had only recently become accessible. It was written originally, however, to discredit the educational practices of a certain person — designated by the pseudonym " Cornificius " — who was offering a short and showy education, and spreading it abroad through his disciples. The description of " Cornificius " and his

school is not necessarily true, but some passages are
quoted from it to illustrate a mode of educational argument thoroughly characteristic of the Middle Ages, —
and not unknown to-day. They also give point, by contrast, to the education and views of John Salisbury himself. John begins by personal abuse of " Cornificius " :

The shamelessness of his looks, the rapacity of his hands,
the frivolousness of his bearing, the foulness of his manners
(which the whole neighborhood spews out), the obscenity of
his lust, the ugliness of his body, the baseness of his life, his
spotted reputation, I would lay bare and thrust into the face of
the public, did not my respect for his Christian name restrain
me. For being mindful of my profession, and of the fraternal
communion which we have in the Lord, I have believed that indulgence should be given to his person while, nevertheless,
indulgence is not given to his sin.

Having fairly joined battle by several pages of vitu-
peration, John proceeds to describe his opponent's manner of teaching :

But I object vigorously to his views, which have destroyed
many, because he has a crowd that believes in him, and although
the new Cornificius is more senseless than the old, yet a mob of
foolish ones agrees with him. And there are in particular
some of these who, although inert and slothful, are eager to
seem rather than to be wise.

. . . .

For my part I am not at all surprised if after being employed
at a large fee, and beating his drum a long time, he taught his
credulous hearer to know nothing. For he, too, was equally
untaught by teachers, since, without eloquence, and yet verbose,
and lacking the fruit of ideas, he continuously throws to the
wind the foliage of words. . . . He feeds his hearers on fables

and trifles, and if what he promises is true, he will make them eloquent without the need of skill, and philosophers by a short cut and without effort. . . . In that school of philosophizers at that time the question whether the pig which is being led to market is held by the man or by the string, was considered insoluble. Also, whether he who bought the whole cloak bought the cowl. Decidedly incongruous was the speech in which these words, " congruous " and " incongruous argument" and " reason " did not make a great noise, with multifold negative particles and transitions through " esse " and " non-esse." . . . A wordy clamor was enough to secure the victory, and he who introduced anything from any source reached the goal of his proposition. . . . Therefore they suddenly became expert philosophers, for he who had come there illiterate delayed in the schools scarcely longer than the time within which young birds get their feathers. So the fresh teachers from the schools and the young birds from the nests flew off together, having lingered an equal length of time. . . . They talked only of congruity or reason, and argument resounded from the lips of all, and to give its common name to an ass, or a man, or any of nature's works, was like a crime, or was much too inelegant or crude, and abhorrent to a philosopher. . . . Hence this seething pot of speech in which the stupid old man exults, insulting those who revere the originators of the Arts because when he pretends to devote his energies to them he finds nothing useful in them.[1]

John's own training was in marked contrast to all this. Instead of remaining in the schools " scarcely longer than the time within which young birds get their feathers," he spent, as above noted, twelve years in study. Instead of devoting himself to logic and disputation alone, he received an extensive training in the classics and in theology. His first teacher at Paris was Abelard.

[1] *Metalogicus*, ed. Giles, I, 2, 3.

When I was a very young man, I went to study in France, the year after the death of that lion in the cause of justice, Henry [the First], king of England.   There I sought out that famous teacher and Peripatetic philosopher of Pallet [Abelard], who at that time presided at Mont St. Genevieve, and was the subject of admiration to all men.   At his feet I received the first rudiments of the dialectic art [logic], and shewed the utmost avidity to pick up and store away in my mind all that fell from his lips.   When, however, much to my regret, Abelard left us, I attended Master Alberic, a most obstinate Dialectician, and unflinching assailant of the Nominal Sect.   Two years I stayed at Mont St. Genevieve, under the tuition of Alberic and Master Robert de Melun.

Then follows a characterization of these teachers. The statement that one of them went to Bologna for the further study of logic indicates that that place was eminent for its teaching of dialectics as well as for the study of law.

One of these teachers was scrupulous even to minutiae, and everywhere found some subject to raise a question; for the smoothest surface presented inequalities to him, and there was no rod so smooth that he could not find a knot in it, and shew how it might be got rid of.   The other of the two was prompt in reply, and never for the sake of subterfuge avoided a question that was proposed; but he would choose the contradictory side, or by multiplicity of words would show that a simple answer could not be given.   In all questions, therefore, he was subtle and profuse, whilst the other in his answer was perspicuous, brief, and to the point.   If two such characters could ever have been united in the same person, he would be the best hand at disputation that our times have produced.   Both of them possessed acute wit, and an indomitable perseverance, and I believe they would have turned out great and distinguished men in Physical Studies, if they had supported themselves on the great base of Literature, and more closely followed the tracks of the ancients, instead of taking such pride in their own discoveries.

All this is said with reference to the time during which I attended on them. For one of them afterwards went to Bologna, and there unlearnt what he had taught: on his return also, he untaught it: whether the change was for the better or the worse, I leave to the judgment of those who heard him before and after. The other of the two was also a proficient in the more exalted Philosophy of Divinity, wherein he obtained a distinguished name.

With these teachers I remained two years, and got so versed in commonplaces, rules, and elements in general, which boys study, and in which my teachers were most weighty, that I seemed to myself to know them as well as I knew my own nails and fingers. There was one thing which I had certainly attained to, namely, to estimate my own knowledge much higher than it deserved. I thought myself a young scholar, because I was ready in what I had been taught.

Evidence external to this narrative shows that he now went to the school at Chartres, — some sixty miles southwest of Paris, — which was one of three great French schools of the period (see p. 10). During the first half of the twelfth century it became famous under the teaching of the brothers Theodoric and Bernard Sylvester, who are both mentioned in the following passages. The school was distinguished in particular for its devotion to Grammar, Rhetoric, and classical Latin literature; in this respect it was in marked contrast to Paris, where Logic and Theology were the prevailing studies.

I then, beginning to reflect and to measure my strength, attended on the Grammarian William de Conches during the space of three years; and read much at intervals: nor shall I ever regret the way in which my time was then spent.   After this I became a follower of Richard l'Eveque, a man who was master of every kind of learning, and whose breast contained much more than his tongue dared give utterance to ; for he had learning rather than eloquence, truthfulness rather than vanity, virtue rather than ostentation.   With him I reviewed all that I had learned from the others, besides certain things, which I now learnt for the first time, relating to the Quadrivium, in which I had already acquired some information from the German Hardewin.   I also again studied Rhetoric, which I had before learnt very superficially with some other studies from Master Theodoric, but without understanding what I read.   Afterwards I learnt it more fully from Peter Hely.[1]

In another chapter, which is here inserted in the narrative, John describes in detail the teaching at Chartres. This is one of the most complete accounts which we have of the manner and the matter of the teaching in a twelfth-century school.   He begins by a general discussion of the importance of Grammar, which is the " foundation and root " of reading, teaching, and reflection.   Throughout this discussion he refers constantly to Quintilian's " Institutes of Oratory."   The study of Rhetoric and of other Arts prepares one for the proper understanding of Literature : " The greater the number of Arts with which one is imbued, and the more fully he is imbued with them, so much the more completely will he appreciate the elegance of the authors, and the more clearly will he teach them."

As to the study of Literature, care should be used in selecting the best authors.   Bernard, he reports, " always said that unnecessary reading should be avoided, and

[1] *Metalogicus*, II, 10.

that the writings of illustrious authors were sufficient; since to study whatever all that the most contemptible men have ever said results in too great torture or in idle boasting, and hinders and even overwhelms the intelligence, which is better left empty for other writings." The reading chosen was classical Latin literature; " in this reverent dependence upon the ancients, lies the main peculiarity of the school of Chartres," which under Bernard and his brother " enjoyed a peculiar distinction, continually growing until it became almost an unapproached pre-eminence among the schools of Gaul." [1]

This reading is in turn a preparation for Philosophy. " He who aspires to Philosophy should understand reading, teaching and reflection, together with practice in good works." " Search Virgil and Lucan, and there, no matter of what philosophy you are professor, you will find it in the making." All this is in marked contrast to the method of " Cornificius," who proposed to train philosophers " suddenly." John continues:

Bernard of Chartres, the most copious source of letters in Gaul in modern times, followed this method, and in the reading of authors showed what was simple, and fell under the ordinary rules; the figures of grammar, the adornments of rhetoric, the quibbles of sophistries; and where the subject of his own lesson suggested reading related to other arts, these matters he brought into full view, yet in such wise that he did not teach everything about each topic but, in proportion to the capacity of his audience, dispensed to them in due time the full scope of the subject. And because the brilliancy of any speech depends either on *Propriety* (that is, the correct agreement of adjective or

[1] Poole, pp. 119, 114.

verb with the substantive) or on *Metathesis* (that is, the transfer
of the meaning of an expression for a worthy reason to another
signification), these were the things which he took every opportunity to inculcate in the minds of his hearers.

And since the memory is strengthened by exercise and the
wits are sharpened by imitating what is heard, he urged some by
warnings, and some by floggings and punishments [to the constant practice of memorizing and imitation].   They were individually required on the following day to reproduce some part
of what they had heard the day before, some more, some less,
for with them the following day was the pupil of the day
preceding.

Evening drill, which was called *declension*, was packed with
so much grammar that if one gave a whole year to it he would
have at his command, if he were not unusually dull, a method of
speaking and writing, and he could not be ignorant of expressions which are in common use. . . . For those of the boys for
whom preliminary exercises in imitating prose or poetry were
prescribed, he announced the poets or orators and bade them
imitate their example, pointing out the way they joined their
words and the elegance of their perorations.

But if any one to make his own work brilliant had borrowed
the cloak of another he detected the theft and convicted him,
though he did not very often inflict a punishment ; but he directed the culprit thus convicted, if the poorness of his work
had so merited, to condescend with modest favor to express the
exact meaning of the author ; and he made the one who imitated
his predecessors worthy of imitation by his successors.

The following matters, too, he taught among the first rudiments and fixed them in their minds : — the value of order ;
what is praiseworthy in embellishment and in [choice of]
words ; where there is tenuity and, as it were, emaciation of
speech ; where, a pleasing abundance ; where, excess ; and
where, a due limit in all things. . . .

And since in the entire preliminary training of those who are
to be taught there is nothing more useful than to grow accus-

tomed to that which must needs be done with skill, they repeatedly wrote prose and poetry every day, and trained themselves by mutual comparisons, — a training than which nothing is more effective for eloquence, nothing more expeditious for learning; and it confers the greatest benefit upon life, at least, if affection [rather than envy] rules these comparisons, if humility is not lost in literary proficiency.[1]

John's stay at Chartres (1138–1141) made him a permanent advocate of liberal education; but to no avail; the influence of Paris and the rising tide of Aristotelianism gained the day. As a champion of the newly-recovered works of Aristotle (see p. 42) he was more in accord with the tendencies of his time.

The concluding section of the account narrates John's return to Paris, his further studies there (1141–1148), and his visit to his old school on the "Mount":

From hence I was withdrawn by the poverty of my condition, the request of my companions, and the advice of my friends, that I should undertake the office of a tutor. I obeyed their wishes; and on my return [to Paris] after three years, finding Master Gilbert [de la Porrée] I studied Logic and Divinity with him: but he was very speedily removed from us, and in his place we had Robert de Poule, a man amiable alike for his rectitude and his attainments. Then came Simon de Poissy, who was a faithful reader, but an obtuse disputator. These two were my teachers in Theology only.

Twelve years having passed away, whilst I was engaged in these various occupations, I determined to revisit my old companions, whom I found still engaged with Logic at Mont St. Genevieve, and to confer with them touching old matters of debate; that we might by mutual comparison measure together our several progress. I found them as before, and where they

[1] *Metalogicus*, I, 24.

3

were before ; nor did they appear to have reached the goal in unravelling the old questions, nor had they added one jot of a proposition. The aims that once inspired them, inspired them still : they had progressed in one point only : they had un-learned moderation, they knew not modesty ; in such wise that one might despair of their recovery. And thus experience taught me a manifest conclusion, that, whereas dialectic furthers other studies, so if it remain by itself it lies bloodless and barren, nor does it quicken the soul to yield fruit of philosophy, except the same conceive from elsewhere.[1]

This was doubtless one of the experiences which led John to vigorous argument on the futility of devotion to Logic alone, and on the importance of a liberal education :

That eloquence is of no effect without wisdom is a saying that is frequent and true. Whence it is evident that to be of effect it operates within the limits of wisdom. Therefore eloquence is effective in proportion to the measure of wisdom which each one has acquired ; for the former does harm if it is dissociated from the latter.

From this it follows that dialectic, which is the quickest and most prompt among the hand-maids of eloquence, is of use to each one in proportion to the measure of his knowledge. For it is of most use to him who knows the most and of least use to him who knows little. For as the sword of Hercules in the hand of a pygmy or dwarf is ineffective, while the same sword in the hand of Achilles or Hector strikes down everything like a thunderbolt, so dialectic, if it is deprived of the vigor of the other disciplines is to a certain degree crippled and almost useless. If it is vigorous through the might of the others, it is powerful in destroying all falsehood and, to ascribe the mini-

[1] *Metalogicus*, II, 10. The translation of this chapter is adapted from Giles, *Works of John of Salisbury*, I, p. xiii, and R. L. Poole, *Illustrations of the History of Mediaeval Thought*, pp. 210, 212.

mum to it, it is adequate for the proper discussion of all things. . . .

Now it is very easy for each workman to talk about his own art ; but to do skilfully what the art requires, is most difficult. For what physician is there who does not talk often and much about elements, and humors, and complexions, and diseases, and the rest that pertain to physic ? But he who gets well on such talk could well have afforded to be even sicker. What ethical teacher has not an abundance of rules for good living so long as they exist only on his lips ? But it is clearly a much harder task to express them in actual life. Mechanics, individually, talk glibly about their own arts, but not one of them so lightly vies (in practice) with the architect or the boxer. It is the same in every other line. So it is very easy to talk about definition, arguments, or genus and the like, but to devise these same things within the limits of a single art for the purpose of performing fully the functions of the art, is far more difficult [i. e. to discuss logic in the abstract is easy, but to reason logically in any specific field of knowledge is difficult]. Therefore he who is hampered by a dearth of the disciplines will not have the power which Dialectic promises and affords.[1]

The views of John of Salisbury concerning the study of Aristotle are indicated on pages 42–44.

2. THE NEW METHOD

The new method of study and investigation, developed by Abelard, was a second influence of importance in the growth of universities. The method itself — later known as the scholastic method — is illustrated on pages 20, 58, 121 ff. The present section therefore merely indicates the ways in which it influenced the course of higher education.

[1] *Metalogicus*, II, 9.

(*a*) The new method was one cause of the awakened interest in study and investigation. Its effect is thus described by the most learned historian of mediaeval universities :

Paris and Bologna experienced before all other schools, and nearly simultaneously, at the beginning of the twelfth century, an unexpected, almost sudden development. For in these schools alone a definite branch of learning was treated . . . by a new method, adapted to contemporary needs, but hitherto unknown, or insufficiently known, to other teachers of the period ; and thereby a new era of scientific investigation was inaugurated. This new method had an attractive power for teachers and scholars of various countries. . . . In this way the cornerstones of permanent abodes of learning were laid. The continually growing number of scholars brought with it the increase of teachers ; the desire of both classes for learning was awakened ; and this desire, and the combative exchange of ideas in the disputations, — which now first became really established in the schools as a result of the new method, — were effective forces to keep investigation active, and the schools themselves from decline.

In Paris, it was the cultivation of Logic, but chiefly the new method in Theology, . . . developed in various ways especially by Abelard and other teachers, and extended by his contemporaries and their disciples . . . which caused the revolution in the schools of that city.[1]

(*b*) The new method of Abelard established a new form of exposition, and consequently a new mode of teaching, in Canon Law and in Theology. The earliest university text-book in Canon Law — the " Decretum" of Gratian — adopted this method, with some

[1] Denifle : *Die Entstehung der Universitäten des Mittelalters*, I, 45, 46.

modifications. It was followed in portions of the chief text-book in Theology, — the " Sentences " of Peter Lombard. Variously modified, it became the method used in all subsequent scholastic philosophy and theology. It was widely used in connection with other university studies. In general, it was to mediaeval education what the method of experiment is to the study and teaching of modern natural science. A good illustration of its recent use is Thomas Harper's " Metaphysic of the School."

(*c*) The scholastic method became the basis of one of the most important university exercises, — the disputation or debate, which was employed in every field of study.[1]

3. THE NEW STUDIES

During the twelfth and thirteenth centuries the intellectual life of western Europe was enriched by the addition of a group of books, old and new, which were destined to influence profoundly the growth of the universities, as well as the whole course of mediaeval life and thought. Without some such addition to the stock of learning higher education could hardly have developed at all, for the materials available for it previous to the twelfth century were decidedly scanty. The books presently to be described furnished a body of advanced and solid instruction, suited to the needs of the times. They formed one of the permanent influences which both developed and maintained centers of

[1] See p. 115. The example given shows also an obvious weakness of the method.

higher education, for the new learning was not less potent in attracting students than the fame of individual teachers or the new method of study.

The greater number of the books which formed the body of university instruction were recoveries from the mass of ancient and long-disused Greek and Roman learning, together with a few works of Arabic and Jewish origin. To this group belong the works of Aristotle, the body of Roman Law, and the medical works of Galen, Hippocrates, and various Arabic and Jewish physicians. In the main, these had been hitherto unknown in western Europe, or at least practically forgotten since the days of the Roman Empire. In the twelfth and thirteenth centuries they were collected and made generally accessible to students. Those not originally written in Latin were now translated into Latin; manuscript copies were multiplied and widely diffused.

But the intellectual activity of the times accomplished much more than the recovery of some fragments of ancient learning; it also created two new fields of study, — Scholastic Philosophy and Theology, and Canon Law, — and produced the text-books which marked them off as distinct and professional studies. The book which established the *method* of these studies was Abelard's "Yes and No" (see p. 20); but the works which furnished the substance of university instruction were, in Theology, the " Sentences " (Sententiae) of Peter Lombard, and in Canon Law, the " Decree " (Decretum) of Gratian, which was also known as the " Harmony of Contradictory Canons " (Concordia Discordantium Canonum), and additions thereto, indicated on page 56.

Thus, during the twelfth and thirteenth centuries, the growth of universities was stimulated by the development of a great body of learning hitherto inaccessible or unknown. The striking nature of this development will be clearer if we recall that no addition to the learning of western Europe in the least degree comparable to this had been made during the entire seven centuries preceding.

The books above mentioned did not constitute the sole resources for higher education. Besides the already long-used text-books on the Seven Liberal Arts there were mathematical and philosophical works of Arabic origin, and as the revival progressed many new books were written on the old subjects. But the books already named were fundamentally important as furnishing not only the early intellectual impulse to the growth of universities, but also the main body of studies in the Faculties of Arts, Theology, Law, and Medicine down to the year 1500. Many of them were in use at a much later date, and some — with many revisions — are still standard text-books. No one can understand the intellectual life of the universities who does not have some acquaintance with the titles and contents of these works. It may be added that acquaintance with them is essential also to the understanding of European history and literature. This section is therefore devoted to certain details concerning the early history of university studies.

(a) *The Works of Aristotle*

The works of Aristotle were composed in Athens, 335–322 B. C. Their history, from the time of Aristotle's death to their appearance in Latin translations in western Europe, fifteen hundred years later, cannot be here detailed. The translations commonly used in the universities were nearly all made during the twelfth and thirteenth centuries. The earlier ones were made in Spain, from Arabic versions of the original Greek; the later, directly from Greek copies found in Constantinople, and elsewhere in the East. The Arabic-Latin translations were very poor, owing to the two removes from the original Greek and the incapacity of the translators. Those directly from the Greek were somewhat better, yet far from satisfactory; and new versions were repeatedly made down to the end of the fifteenth century. University reforms sometimes included the adoption of these better translations (see p. 48).

The works known by the year 1300 may be classified in four groups:

I. Logical treatises commonly referred to as the Organon or Methodology.	1. Categories	=	{Predicamenta. Categoriae.
	2. On Interpretation	=	{De Interpretatione. Peri Hermeneias.
	3. Prior Analytics	=	Analytica Priora.
	4. Posterior Analytics	=	Analytica Posteriora.
	5. Topics	=	Topica.
	6. Sophistical Refutations	=	Sophisticae Elenchi.
II. Moral and Practical Philosophy.	7. Politics.		
	8. Ethics.		
	9. Rhetoric.		
	10. Poetics.		

III. Natural
Philosophy.
11. A Physical Discourse (Physics).
12. On the Heavens.
13. On Generation and Destruction.
14. Meteorologics.
15. Researches about Animals.
16. On Parts of Animals.
17. On Locomotion of Animals.
18. On Generation of Animals.
19. On the Soul.
20. Appendices to the work " On the Soul."
  (*a*) On Sense and Sensible Things.
  (*b*) On Memory and Recollection.
  (*c*) On Sleep and Waking.
  (*d*) On Dreams and Prophesying in Sleep.
  (*e*) On Longevity and Shortlivedness.
  (*f*) On Youth and Old Age.
  (*g*) On Life and Death.
  (*h*) On Respiration.

IV. Rational
Philosophy.
21. Metaphysics.

This encyclopedic collection became accessible in Latin translations only by slow degrees.   Abelard knew only the first two (possibly also the third and fourth) works of the Organon.   John of Salisbury, in the next generation, was familiar with the six treatises of the Organon, but apparently not with the others.   Little seems to have been added to these until the beginning of the thirteenth century, when the Ethics, the Physics, and the Metaphysics were mentioned at Paris, — the last two as forbidden works.   The great era of translation seems to have been between 1200 and 1270, when both Arabic-Latin and Greek-Latin versions were made of most of the remaining treatises.   The recovery of Aristotle thus occupied more than a century and a half.   During that period the intellectual life of western Europe was stimulated by the influx of hitherto unknown works of that philosopher, and weighty additions were made to the list of available studies.

As usual, the world of scholars and the universities were slow to recognize the worth of the new studies. This was due partly to the natural conservatism of teachers, and partly to the fear of ecclesiastical authorities that the study of Aristotle would give rise to heresies.   Thus in the documents of the time we meet, on the one hand, vigorous arguments by progressive scholars in favor of Aristotle, and on the other, university regulations prescribing what books shall or shall not be studied.

The attitude of Abelard toward Aristotle has already been cited (see p. 19).

His pupil, John of Salisbury, devotes a considerable portion of the *Metalogicus* to a discussion of the utility of the various portions of the Organon and to the defense of Aristotle, as is shown by the titles of various chapters of that work.   It is important to remember that he is advocating the study of the *newly* translated books, as well as those already known:

That Logic, because it seeks the truth, takes the lead in all Philosophy.

On the usefulness of the Categories and their appliances.

What Conception is, and the usefulness of the Periermeniae or more correctly Periermenia. [Peri Hermeneias. On Interpretation.]

Of what the Body of Art consists ; and on the usefulness of the Topics.

Why Aristotle deserved more than others the name of philosopher.

That Aristotle erred in many ways ; that he is eminent in Logic.

John of Salisbury clearly recognized the supremacy of Aristotle among logicians. After naming Apuleius, Cicero, Porphyry, Boethius, Augustine, and others, he adds :

But while individually they shine forth because of their own merits, they all boast that they worship the very footsteps of Aristotle ; to such a degree, indeed, that by a sure pre-eminence he has made peculiarly his own the common name of all philosophers. For by Antonomy [a figure of speech] he is called The Philosopher *par excellence.*

It is clear, however, that Aristotle had by no means attained, at the middle of the twelfth century, the authoritative position which he held a hundred years later. This appears in the chapter " On those who Carp at the Works of Aristotle " :

I cannot sufficiently wonder what sort of a mind they have (if, that is, they have any) who carp at the works of Aristotle, which, in any case, I proposed not to expound but to praise. Master Theodoric, as I recall, ridiculed the Topics, — not of Aristotle, but of Drogo. Yet he once taught those very Topics. Certain auditors of Master Robert of Melun calumniated this work as practically useless. All decried the Categories. Where-fore I hesitated some time about commending . them ; but [there was no question as to] the rest of his works, since they were commended by the judgment of all ; but I did not think that they should be praised grudgingly. Yet opposition is made to the Elenchi [Sophistical Refutations], though stupidly, because it contains poetry; but clearly the idiom of [the Greek] language does not lend itself readily to translation.   In this respect the Analytics seem to me preferable, because they are no less efficient for actual use, and because by their easier comprehension they stimulate eloquence.[1]

The slowness with which these works made their way is described by Roger Bacon at the end of the thirteenth century.

But a part of the philosophy of Aristotle has come slowly into the use of the Latins.   For his Natural Philosophy and Metaphysics, and the Commentaries of Averrhoes and of others, were translated in our times, and were excommunicated at Paris before the year of our Lord 1237 on account of [their heretical views on] the eternity of matter and of time, and on account of the [heresies contained in the] book on Interpretation of Dreams (which is the third book on Sleep and Wakefulness), and on account of the many errors in the translation.   The Logicalia were also slowly received and read, for the blessed Edmund, Archbishop of Canterbury, was the first at Oxford, in my time, to lecture on the book of Elenchi [Sophistical Refutations] and I saw Master Hugo who at first read the book of Posterior Analytics, and I saw his opinion.   So there were few [books] which were considered worth [reading] in the aforesaid philosophy of Aristotle, considering the multitudes of Latins; nay, exceedingly few and almost none, up to this year of our Lord 1292. So, too, the Ethics of Aristotle has been tardily tried and has lately been read by Masters, though only here and there.   And the entire remaining philosophy of Aristotle in a thousand volumes, in which he treated all the knowledges, has never yet been translated and made known to the Latins.[2]

[1] John of Salisbury, *Metalogicus*, IV, 24.
[2] Document printed by Rashdall, Vol. II, Pt. II, p. 754.

The last sentence of the account displays an ignorance of the number of Aristotle's extant writings which was doubtless shared by all of Bacon's contemporaries. Earlier writers, beginning with Andronicus of Rhodes (first century B. C.), had also placed the number at one thousand; Bacon probably copied the statement from one of these.

The attitude of ecclesiastical authorities toward the study of Aristotle at Paris is expressed in a series of regulations extending over nearly half a century (1210–1254). They indicate at first a fear of certain of the newly translated books on account of their heretical views, as is stated by Roger Bacon (p. 44). This suspicion gradually disappears; and by 1254 all the more important works of Aristotle are not only approved, but prescribed for study.

In 1210 a church council held at Paris sentenced certain heretics to be burned, condemned various theological writings, and added:

Nor shall the books of Aristotle on Natural Philosophy, and the Commentaries [of Averrhoes on Aristotle] be read in Paris in public or in secret; and this we enjoin under pain of excommunication.[1]

In 1215 the statutes of the Papal Legate, Robert de Courçon, for the University, prescribe in detail what shall, and what shall not, be studied:

The treatises of Aristotle on Logic, both the Old and the New, are to be read in the schools in the regular and not in the extraordinary courses. On feast-days [holidays] nothing is to

[1] Chart. Univ. Paris., I, No. 11, p. 73.

be read except . . . the Ethics, if one so chooses, and the fourth book of the Topics. The books of Aristotle on Metaphysics or Natural Philosophy, or the abridgments of these works, are not to be read.[1]

In other words, the Old and New Logic are prescribed studies; the Ethics, and Topics, Bk. IV, are optional; the Metaphysics and the Natural Philosophy are forbidden.

Sixteen years later (1231) the Statutes of Pope Gregory IX for the University prohibit only the Natural Philosophy, and even these works only until they are " purged from error ":

Furthermore, we command that the Masters of Arts . . shall not use in Paris those books on Natural Philosophy which for a definite reason were prohibited in the provincial council [of 1210], until they have been examined and purged from every suspicion of error.[2]

The final triumph of Aristotle in the University is indicated by the statute of the Masters of Arts in 1254.[3] It must have had at least the tacit approval of the pope or his delegate. The statute is too long to quote effectively to the point. None of the works are forbidden, and a large number are prescribed. The list of works mentioned includes —

(1) The six logical treatises of the Organon; (2) Ethics, Bks. I–IV; (3) Physics, On the Heavens and the Earth, Meteorologics, On Generation, On Animals, On the Soul, On Sense and Sensible Things, On Sleep and Waking, On Memory and Recollection, On Life and Death; (4) Metaphysics. To these are added two other

[1] *l. c.* No. 20, p. 78.   [2] *l. c.* No. 79.   [3] *l. c.* No. 246.

works then believed to be Aristotle's, — On Plants, and
On Causes, — and numerous books by other authors
(named on p. 137) which do not concern the present discussion. A comparison of the list above with the list on
page 40 will show that neauly the whole range of Aristotle's works is prescribed. Comparison with the statute
of 1215 will show not only a change of view regarding
the works then forbidden, but also an immense broaden-
ing of the studies of the Faculty of Arts in the course of
forty years.

The foregoing details are cited to give an idea of the
first stage of the question of Aristotle in the universities.
The statute of 1254 may be taken as closing the long
struggle for the recognition of his works. The broad
principle of their general acceptance had been established; thenceforward for nearly three centuries they
remained the dominant studies of the Faculties of Arts
everywhere.

These centuries include the second period of their
academic history. Their authority is now hardly ques-
tioned; and woe to the questioner! They furnish the
basis for the great structure of scholastic philosophy;
they are reconciled with Christian doctrine. Aristotle
is thenceforward "The Philosopher" — he is so styled
even in modern scholastic philosophy; he is "the fore-
runner of Christ in things natural," "the master of those
who know." In this period, then, academic debate concerned itself with matters of detail. What portions of
his works should be studied for the various degrees in
Arts? In what order should they be studied? What
comments should be read? What translations should

be used? So late as 1519 these are the chief questions considered in the reformed plan of studies in Arts at Leipzig. The reader will note the stress laid upon the study of the text itself; the exclusion of frivolous comments, and the use of the latest translations by Greek scholars.

Inasmuch as no good thing is more desirable than philosophy, as Cicero says, and none more advantageous has been given to the race of mortals, or granted by heaven, or will ever be given as a gift; in order that we may possess this too, we choose as our guide Aristotle, whom we cause to be commended for his knowledge of facts, the number of his works, his ability in speaking, and the acumen of his intellectual powers. Nor will we interpret the visions and involved questions of his interpreters, since it is characteristic of a very poor intellect to grow wise from commentaries only, in which, neglecting Aristotle's meaning, the Sophists dispute about empty trifles. But his works, translated in part by Archeropylus [Argyropulos], in part by Augustus Nipho and Hermolaus Barbarus and Theodorus Gaza, will be made clear in the order outlined below:[1] [Then follows the list of books, for which see p. 134].

The third stage of the debate concerning Aristotle began shortly after 1500. His works were less exclusively the subject of study: they were being displaced by the Latin and Greek classics. They were, moreover, the object of repeated attack. In 1536, in the University of Paris, which had so long maintained their study, Pierre Ramus successfully defended the startling thesis, "Everything that Aristotle taught is false." This was only one sign of their loss of prestige. New and improved text-books in Logic absorbed the useful portions

[1] Zarncke, *Statutenbücher der Universität Leipzig*, p. 39.

of the Organon; the authority of the Natural Philosophy waned with the rise of experimental science; that of the Metaphysics yielded to the new philosophy of Descartes. By the end of the seventeenth century they ceased to be a potent factor in university studies.

(b) *The Roman Law*

The great compilation of the Roman Law known as the *Corpus Juris Civilis* (Body of Civil Law) constitutes a second important addition of the twelfth century to the field of university studies. It was probably more important as an influence upon the growth of universities than the works of Aristotle.

The greater part of the Corpus Juris was compiled at Constantinople, 529–533 A. D., by certain eminent jurists under the Roman Emperor, Justinian. The purpose of the work was to reduce to order and harmony the mass of confused and contradictory statutes and legal opinions, and to furnish a standard body of laws of manageable size in place of the unwieldly mass of incorrect texts commonly in use, so that " the entire ancient law, in a state of confusion for some fourteen hundred years and now by us made clear, may be, so to speak, enclosed within a wall and have nothing left outside it." The jurists entrusted with this work were also required to prepare an introductory book for students, as described below. After the completion of the whole work Justinian issued (533–565) many new statutes (Novellae) which were never officially collected, but which came to be considered a part of the Corpus Juris. The main divisions of the Body of Civil Law are —

4

(1) The Code, in twelve books, which contains statutes of the Emperors from the third century A. D.

Since [says Justinian] we find the whole course of our statutes . . . to be in a state of such confusion that they reach to an infinite length and surpass the bounds of all human capacity, it was therefore our first desire to make a beginning with the most sacred Emperors of old times, to amend their statutes, and to put them in a clear order, so that they might be collected together in one book, and, being divested of all superfluous repetition and most inequitable disagreement, might afford to all mankind the ready resource of their unalloyed character.[1]

(2) The Digest, or Pandects, in fifty books, containing extracts from the opinions of Roman lawyers on a great variety of legal questions. This work was also undertaken to bring order and harmony out of the prevailing confusion:

We have entrusted the entire task to Tribonianus, a most distinguished man, Master of the Offices, ex-quaestor of our sacred palace, and ex-consul, and we have laid on him the whole service of the enterprise described, so that with other illustrious and learned colleagues he might fulfil our desire. [He is] to collect together and to submit to certain modifications the very most important works of old times, thoroughly intermixed and broken up as they may almost be called. But in the midst of our careful researches, it was intimated to us by the said exalted person that there were nearly two thousand books written by the old lawyers, and more than three million lines were left us by them, all of which it was requisite to read and carefully consider and out of them to select whatever might be best. [This was accomplished] so that everything of great importance was collected into fifty books, and all ambiguities were settled, without any refractory passage being left.[2]

[1] *Digest*, translated by C. H. Monro, p. xiii (preface to *Code*).
[2] *l. c.* pp. xxv, xxvi.

In mediaeval university documents the Digest is frequently mentioned in three divisions, which probably indicate three separate instalments in which the MS. of the work was brought to Bologna in the eleventh and twelfth centuries: the Old Digest (Digestum Vetus) Bks. I–XXIV, title ii, Infortiatum Bks. XXIV, title iii–XXXVIII, title iii, and New Digest (Digestum Novum) Bks. XXXVIII, title iv–L. The meaning of the term Infortiatum is uncertain.

This distinction between the various parts of the Digest is purely arbitrary. . . . The division must have originated in an accidental separation of some archetypal MS.[1]

(3) The Institutes, in four books, an elementary text-book for students. The purpose of the book was to afford a simple, clear, and trustworthy introduction to the study of law, and to economize the student's time:

When we had arranged and brought into perfect harmony the hitherto confused mass of imperial constitutions (i. e. the Code), we then extended our care to the vast volumes of ancient law ; and, sailing as it were across the mid ocean, have now completed, through the favour of heaven, a work that once seemed beyond hope (i. e. the Digest).

When by the blessing of God this task was accomplished, we summoned the most eminent Tribonian, master and ex-quaestor of our palace, together with the illustrious Theophilus and Dorotheus, professors of law, all of whom have on many occasions proved to us their ability, legal knowledge, and obedience to our orders ; and we have specially charged them to compose, under our authority and advice, Institutes, so that you may no more learn the first elements of law from old and erroneous sources, but apprehend them by the clear light of imperial wis-

1 Rashdall, I, 208.

dom ; and that your minds and ears may receive nothing that
is useless or misplaced, but only what obtains in actual practice.
So that, whereas, formerly, the junior students could scarcely,
after three years' study, read the imperial constitutions, you may
now commence your studies by reading them, you who have
been thought worthy of an honour and a happiness so great
that the first and last lessons in the knowledge of the law should
issue for you from the mouth of the emperor.

When, therefore, by the assistance of the same eminent person Tribonian and that of other illustrious and learned men, we
had compiled the fifty books, called Digests or Pandects, in
which is collected the whole ancient law, we directed that these
Institutes should be divided into four books, which might serve
as the first elements of the whole science of law.

In these books a brief exposition is given of the ancient laws,
and of those also, which, overshadowed by disuse, have been
again brought to light by our imperial authority.

These four books of Institutes thus compiled, from all the
Institutes left us by the ancients, and chiefly from the commentaries of our Gaius, both in his Institutes and in his work on
daily affairs, and also from many other commentaries, were presented to us by the three learned men we have above named.
We have read and examined them and have accorded to them
all the force of our constitutions.

Receive, therefore, with eagerness, and study with cheerful
diligence, these our laws, and show yourselves persons of such
learning that you may conceive the flattering hope of yourselves
being able, when your course of legal study is completed, to
govern our empire in the different portions that may be entrusted to your care.

Given at Constantinople on the eleventh day of the calends
of December, in the third consulate of the Emperor Justinian,
ever August (533).[1]

---

[1] Preface to the *Institutes ;* translated by T. C. Sandars, published by
Longmans, Green & Co.

(4) The Novellae (Novels), or new statutes issued by Justinian between the final edition of the Code and his death (534–565). These are really a continuation of the Code, but they were never officially collected.

The Code and the Institutes were known and studied in Italy throughout the Dark Ages, but the Digest, much the largest and most important part of the Corpus Juris, was almost wholly neglected, if not unknown, until the time of Irnerius of Bologna (*c*. 1070–1130). He and his co-laborers collected and arranged the scattered parts of the entire Body of Civil Law, and in particular introduced the Digest to western Europe. "Without the Digest the study of Roman Law was in a worse position than the study of Aristotle when he was known only from the Organon." In a most important sense, therefore, the recovery of the Corpus Juris was a contribution of the twelfth century to the group of available higher studies. Hitherto Law had been taught usually as a mere branch of Rhetoric, and as a part of a liberal education. The body of material now made available was sufficient to occupy the student's entire time for several years. It therefore attained standing as an independent subject, and as a distinctly professional study.

The effect of this newly recovered body of learning upon the rise of universities was very much like that of Abelard and his new method. Students flocked in thousands to study law at Bologna, and toward the close of the twelfth century the University was organized. Numerous other universities arose directly from the same impulse, and " Law was the leading Faculty in by far the greater number of mediaeval universities " (Rash-dall). Except for Canon Law, the Corpus Juris Civilis remained the chief study of the Faculties of Law for more than five centuries. Roman Law is still very generally taught in European universities. Thus the impulse given by Irnerius and his co-laborers is influential in university affairs of to-day.

The influence of Roman Law upon the social and political history of Europe is far-reaching. The subject is beyond the limits of the present work; but it is to be noted that this influence was exerted as a result of its study in the universities (see Rashdall, Vol. II, Pt. II, pp. 708–709).

Rashdall and Denifle think that the example of Justinian inspired the first mediaeval grant of special privileges to scholars (see p. 82). If this is true, the Roman Law had a most important effect upon the history of universities themselves. Two important mediaeval privileges for masters and scholars were exemption from taxation and the right of trial before special courts. Whether or not these were copied from the Roman Law is a question; but the Code of Justinian, following the statutes of earlier emperors, explicitly grants both of these privileges to teachers. These are so often mentioned that it is worth while to present those bearing on the subject:

THE EMPERORS LEO AND ZENO, AUGUSTI, TO EUSEBIUS, MASTER OF OFFICES.

By this law we decree that those who serve in the individual schools, and who, after completing the curricula of their duties, shall have reached the rank of chiefs and through the adored purple of our divinity have won the dignity of most illustrious Counts, shall enjoy both the girdle and all the privileges open to them, and hereafter to their life's end shall be subject to the court of Your Highness only, nor shall they be compelled by the command of any one else whomsoever to undergo civil litigation.

Yet in criminal suits and in matters connected with public tribute we wish the appropriate jurisdiction of the rulers of the provinces to be recognized against even such men, lest, under the pretext of a granted privilege, either the influence of the wicked be increased or the public good be diminished.[1]

THE EMPEROR CONSTANTINE, AUGUSTUS, TO THE PEOPLE.

We direct that physicians, and chiefly imperial physicians, and ex-imperial physicians, grammarians and other professors of letters, together with their wives and sons, and whatever property they possess in their own cities, be immune from all payment of taxes and from all civil or public duties, and that in the provinces they shall not have strangers quartered on them, or perform any official duties, or be brought into court, or be subject to legal process, or suffer injustice ; and if any one harass them he shall be punished at the discretion of the Judge. We also command that their salaries and fees be paid, so that they may more readily instruct many in liberal studies and the above mentioned Arts.

Proclaimed on the fifth day before the Kalends of October (Sept. 27) at Constantinople, in the Consulship of Dalmatius and Zenophilas.[2]

(c) *Canon Law*

About 1142 (the year of Abelard's death) Gratian, a monk of Bologna, doubtless influenced by the school of Roman Law in that city, made a compilation of the Canon Law, which included the canons or rules governing the Church in its manifold activities, — " its relations

[1] *Code*, Bk. 12 ; 29, 2.
[2] A. D. 333, *Code*, Bk. 10 ; 53, 6.

with the secular power, its own internal administration, or the conduct of its members." Hitherto Canon Law had been regarded as merely a subdivision of Theology, just as Roman Law had been considered a branch of Rhetoric. It now became an independent subject, — a further addition to the body of higher studies. As an influence upon the development of universities it was not less important than the *Corpus Juris Civilis*.

The compilation made by Gratian was added to in later generations, and the whole body of church law was known in the fifteenth century as the *Corpus Juris Canonici* (Body of Canon Law). Its main divisions are :

1. The Decree of Gratian (*Decretum Gratiani*) in three parts, published c. 1142. Part I contains one hundred and one distinctions (*distinctiones*) or divisions, which treat of matters relating to ecclesiastical persons and offices. Dist. XXXVII is translated below. Part II contains thirty-six cases (*causae*) each of which is divided into questions (*quaestiones*). These questions deal with problems which may arise in the administration of the canon law. Part III contains five distinctions which deal with the ritual and the sacraments of the church. Under each distinction, or question, are arranged the canons — the views of ecclesiastical authorities — on the matter under discussion.

2 The Decretals (*Decretales*), in five books, published by Pope Gregory IX in 1234.

3. The Sixth Book (*Liber Sextus*), a supplement to the Decretals by Pope Boniface VIII, 1298.

4. The Constitutions of Clementine (*Constitutiones Clementinae*), 1317.

5. Several collections of papal laws not included in those above, known by the general title of *Extravagantes*, i. e., laws *extra vagantes*, or outside of, the four compilations just mentioned.

Among all these the *Decretum* of Gratian was the great innovation which first marked out Canon Law as a distinct field of learning, separate from both Theology and Roman Law. It was written as a text-book; " it was one of those great text-books which take the world by storm." It created an entirely new class of students, separate from those devoted to Arts, Theology, Roman Law, and Medicine, — just as the development of Engineering and other new professional studies have created new groups of university students to-day, — and thereby increased the resort to the universities.

The selection following illustrates numerous characteristics of mediaeval university study. (1) The question itself is a very ancient subject of debate; the controversy, on religious grounds, concerning the study of the classics, had already continued for nearly a thousand years, and was destined to continue for centuries after the appearance of the *Decretum*. Many such questions were debated in the universities for generations. The debate on the classics still rages, though the arguments pro and con no longer raise the point of their influence on religious belief. (2) The selection is one among many examples of the powerful influence of Abelard's method in mediaeval writing and teaching. The reader will at once see in it the form of the " Yes and No." (3) It gives a very good idea of the substance of a university lecture, which would ordinarily consist in reading the actual text and comments here set down (see p. 111). (4) It shows how the mass of comments came to overshadow the original text, and by consequence to absorb the greater part of the attention of teachers and students.   One object of university reform in all studies at the end of the fifteenth and the beginning of the sixteenth century was to sweep away this burdensome and often useless material, and to return to the study of the text itself (see p. 48).   (5)   It illustrates a common mode of interpreting in a figurative sense passages from the Bible which to the modern reader seem to have no figurative meaning.   Thus (pp. 64, 66) the plagues of frogs and flies which Moses brought upon Egypt typify " the empty garrulousness of dialecticians, and their sophistical arguments "; the gifts of the three Magi to the infant Jesus signify " the three parts of philosophy," etc.   Mediaeval literature contains a great mass of such interpretations.

The text and the " gloss," or commentary, are here placed on opposing pages for the sake of clearness. The text is a compilation, chiefly from earlier compilations; Gratian did not as a rule consult the sources themselves.   His pupil, Paucapalea, made many additions to the text, one of which appears in this selection. The gloss here translated is the standard commentary (*glossa ordinaria*) which was used for centuries in the regular university lectures (see p. 108).   Like the text, it is a compilation from many sources.   It was first made (c. 1212) by John the German (Joannes Teutonicus), who added his own notes — usually signed " John " — to his selections from earlier glossators.   The names or titles, often abbreviated, of commentators whom he quotes are frequently appended to their notes, e. g. John of Fa[ënza], Hugo [of Pisa], C[ardinalis], Lau[rentius Hispanus]; many notes are unsigned.

About 1238 the compilation of John the German was revised and enlarged by Bartholomew of Brescia, who also added comments from other writers, e. g. Arc [hidiaconus]. This revision forms the greater part, if not the whole, of the gloss which appears below.

The cross-references, in the comments below, are left untranslated. They are mainly citations of other passages in the *Decretum* itself. Such references as XVI. quaest. III. nemo are to be read, Case XVI, question III, in the section beginning *Nemo ;* XLVIII dist. sit rector means Distinction XLVIII, in the section beginning *Sit rector.* Several of the references in this selection are incorrect.

The gloss on this page belongs to the first line of text on page 60. It forms, with the Summaries on later pages, a complete analysis of the text. It indicates, first, the five subdivisions of the *distinctio ;* second, its general purport. Later summaries analyze small portions of the text. (Cf. the description of the lecture by Odofredus, p. 111.)

This division is divided into five sections ; the second begins : " Then why . . . " (p. 68); the third begins : " The report has come to us " (p. 74) ; the fourth begins : " Christians are forbidden " (p. 75) ; the fifth begins : " As therefore is evident " (p. 75). John of Fa.

* Summary. Here follows the thirty-seventh division in which the question is asked whether it is fitting that the clergy be made acquainted with profane literature, that is, the books of the heathen. And first he proves that they should not be read (as far as " But on the other hand," p. 64). Then he proves the opposite and afterwards gives the solution (to " Then why," p. 68). The first two chapters are plain.

Exodus, XVII. C.

[SHALL PRIESTS BE ACQUAINTED WITH PROFANE LITERATURE, OR NO?]

* But the question (*h*) is asked whether these men should be made acquainted with profane literature.

Here is what is written upon the matter in the fourth Carthaginian Council:

A Bishop should not read the books of the (*i*) heathen.

A bishop should not read the books of the heathen: those of heretics he may read carefully, either of necessity (*k*) or for some special reason.

So Jerome to Pope Damasus on the prodigal son:

Priests are blameworthy who, to the neglect of the Gospels, read comedies.

We see priests of God, to the neglect of the Gospels and the Prophets, reading comedies, singing the Amatory words of bucolic verses, keeping Vergil in their hands, and making that which occurs with boys as a necessity (*k*) ground for accusation against themselves because they do it for pleasure.

Idem:

They walk in the vanity and darkness of the senses who occupy themselves with profane learning.*

Does he not seem to you to be walking in the vanity of the senses, and in darkness of mind, who day and night torments himself with the dialectic art; who, as an investigator of nature, raises his eyes athwart the heavens and, beyond the depths of lands and the abyss, is plunged into the so-called void; who grows warm over iambics, who, in his over zealous mind, analyses and combines the great jungle of metres; and, (to pass to another phase of the matter), who seeks riches by fair means and foul means, who fawns upon kings, grasps at the inheritances of others, and amasses wealth though he knows not at the time to whom he is going to leave it?

(*h*) In this thirty-seventh division Gratian asks (*b*) whether one who is to be ordained ought to be acquainted with profane literature. First, however, he shows that the clergy ought not to give attention to the books of the heathen. (*c*) Then he gives the argument on the other side and offers this solution, that some read the books of the heathen for amusement and pleasure, and this is forbidden, while some read for instruction, and this is lawful, in order that, through these books they may know how to speak correctly and to distinguish the true from the false. John, as far as "Then why" (p. 68). And notice that in all the chapters up to "But on the other hand" (p. 64) pleasure alone seems to be forbidden.

(*i*) Therefore they ought not to hear the laws, for it is a disgrace to them if they wish to be versed in forensic training. C. de testa consulta divalia. But, on the other hand, the laws are divinely promulgated through the mouths of princes as XVI. quaest. III, nemo. (*d*) Some say that it is lawful to hear the laws in order that through them the canons may be better understood. He argues in favor of this division in the section beginning "Some read profane literature" (p. 70). John.

(*k*) In order that they may know how to speak correctly.

* Summary. Four classes of men are blamed under this caption, i. e. dialecticians, who wrestle daily with the dialectic art ; and physicists, who raise their eyes athwart the heavens; and versifiers ; and the avaricious, who acquire wealth by fair means and foul, though at the time they know not to whom they are going to leave it.

(*b*) I. e., incidentally H u g o. Whether the clergy can give attention to the books of the heathen.

(*c*) And he does this as far as the paragraph, " But on the other hand," (p. 66).

(*d*) To the same effect C. de long. tem. praescript l. fin. XXV. quaest. I. ideo. Arc.

Likewise [Jerome] on Isaiah:

He who misunderstands the sacred scriptures, or makes a wrong use of profane wisdom, is drunken with wine * and with strong drink.

They are drunken with wine who (*l*) misunderstand the sacred scriptures and pervert them, and through strong drink they make a wrong use of profane wisdom and the wiles of the dialecticians, which are to be called, not so much wiles as figures, that is, symbols, so-called, and images, which quickly pass away and are destroyed.   Likewise, in accordance with tropology (*m*), we ought to regard as false prophets those who interpret the words of the scriptures otherwise than as the Holy Spirit utters them, and as divine those who from the inferences of their own minds and apart from the authority of divine words, proclaim as true the uncertain events of the future.   Likewise, those who do not understand the Scriptures according to the actual truth eat sour grapes.

Likewise [Jerome] in the Epistle to the Ephesians:

Bishops are blamed who train their own sons in profane literature.*

Let those bishops and priests read [this] who train their own sons in profane literature, and have them read those well-known comedies and sing the base writings of the actors of farces, having educated them perhaps on the money of the church. (*a*)   And that which a virgin, or a widow, or any poor person whatever had offered, pouring out her whole substance as an offering for sin, this [is devoted] to a gift (*b*) of the calendar, and a saturnalian offering, (*c*) and, on the part of the grammarian and orator, to a thank-offering to Minerva, or else it is turned over for domestic expenses, or as a temple donation, or for base gain.   Eli, the priest, was himself holy, but because

* Summary. Under this caption Jerome set forth five cases. For he says that they are drunken with wine who misunderstand and pervert the sacred scriptures. Secondly, they are drunken with strong drink who make a wrong use of profane wisdom. Thirdly, he sets forth who should be called false prophets. Fourthly, who are divine. Fifthly, that he eats sour grapes who expounds the scriptures otherwise than according to the truth, even though it be not contrary to the faith.

(*l*) The ears of those who misunderstand the words of the Master should be cut off : as XXIV. quaest. I. si Petrus.

The ears of those who misunderstand should be torn off.

(*m*) That is, in accordance with the moral meaning, from trope, i. e. a turning (*c*) or application, when we apply our words to the shaping of character.

Tropology.

(*c*) And *logos*, speech, whence, *tropologia*, i. e. the [moral] application of the language. Hugo. As to this see 76 dist. jejunium. in fin.

XLIII. distinct. sit rector.

Additio. They did the opposite and he writes of penitence, distinct. I. super tribus. Archi.

* Summary. In this section those priests are blamed by Jerome, who cause their sons and nephews to read comedies and the verses of the poets ; because also to this purpose and to other base purposes they divert the money of the church. Wherefore he says that such priest should be punished as was Eli who fell prostrate from his seat and died because he did not correct his sons. The statements which follow are clear as far as paragraph " But on the other hand " (p. 64).

(*a*) He argues contrariwise in dist. XXXI. omnino.

(*b*) Strena, — the first gift which is given at the beginning of the Calendar. It is given for a good omen. XXV. quaest. ulti. non observetis.

I King. II. C.

It is called Strena as if from sine threna, i. e. without lamentation.

(*c*) Sportula (a gift) which is given for fables of Saturn, or for celebrating the festival he trained not his sons (*d*) in every form of improving discipline, he fell prostrate and died.

(Also from the replies of Pope Urban to Charles, Chapt. 48).

Palea [Paucapalea, a pupil of Gratian]:

Heretics, when disputing,† place the whole strength of their wits upon the dialectic art, which, in the judgment of philosophers, is defined as having the power not of aiding but of destroying study. But the dialectic art was not pleasing † to God the Father, Son, and Holy Spirit, for the Kingdom of God is in the simplicity of faith, not in contentious speech.

Also Rabanus on the Afflictions of the Church :

The blessed Jerome is beaten by an angel because he was reading the works of Cicero.

We read about the blessed Jerome that when he was reading the works (*e*) of Cicero he was chidden by an angel because, being a Christian man, he was devoting himself to the productions of the pagans.

[The discussion which follows, to " Hence Bede," etc., p. 66, is attributed, in modern editions, to Gratian.]

Hence, too, the prodigal son in the Gospel is blamed because he would fain have filled his belly with the husks (*f*) which the swine did eat.

Hence, too, Origen understands by the flies and frogs with which the Egyptians were smitten, the empty garrulousness of the dialecticians and their sophistical arguments.

From all which instances it is gathered that knowledge of profane literature is not to be sought after by churchmen.

But, on the other hand * one reads that Moses and Daniel were learnèd in all the wisdom of the Egyptians and Chaldeans.

One reads also that God ordered the sons of Israel to spoil (*g*) the Egyptians of their gold and silver; the moral interpretation of this teaches that should we find in the poets either the gold of wisdom or the silver of eloquence, we should turn it to the profit of useful learning. In Leviticus also we are ordered to of Saturn, or for games of Saturn, — for good luck.

(*d*) Such a one is rejected by the evidence, as VI. quaest. I. qui crimen. Also, he cannot be a bishop. As XLVIII. dist. § necesse. Nay he is called a dog rather than a bishop. As II. quaest. VII. qui nec. John.

† Another reading: in their disputations.

† Another reading: "It pleased God to save his people for his Kingdom" &c.

(*e*) Because he read them for pleasure not for instruction, as de conse. dist. V. non mediocriter.

(*f*) That is, with profane wisdom which fills but does not satisfy. (*a*)

(*a*) For as husks load the belly and fill it but do not satisfy, so also this wisdom does not free from spiritual hunger nor banish blindness. But it oppresses with the weight of sins and with the guilt of hell. Whoever therefore, for the removing of the blindness of ignorance seeks to learn other arts and knowledge desires to fill his belly, as it were, with husks. According to Hugo.

* Summary. From now on, Gratian shows that the clergy ought to be learned in profane knowledge. And this is shown from six considerations. The first is stated at the beginning. The second begins: "One reads also." The third begins: "In Leviticus." The fourth begins: "The Magi, too." The fifth begins: "Finally." The sixth begins: "Hence also Ambrose."

(*g*) XIIII. quaest. V. dixit.

Dan. I. a. Exodi III. & XI.

offer up to God the first fruits of honey, that is, the sweetness of human eloquence. The Magi, too, offered three gifts, by which some would have us understand the three parts (h) of philosophy.

[The reader will note that the two paragraphs following belong more properly to the first part of the argument ; they may be inserted just before the third paragraph above, — " From all which instances," etc.]

Finally in his exposition of the Psalms, Cassiodorus bears witness that all the splendor of rhetorical eloquence, all the melody of poetic speech, whatever variety there may be of pleasing pronunciation, have their origin in divine Scriptures.

Hence also Ambrose says concerning the Epistle to the Colossians : The sum total of celestial knowledge or of earthly creation is in Him who is their Fountain-head and Author, so that he who knows Him should not seek anything beyond, because He is goodness and wisdom in their completeness ; whatever is sought elsewhere, in Him is found in its completeness. In Daniel and Solomon he shows that He is for infidels the source of all their eloquence and wisdom. Infidels do not so think, because they do not, in the Gospels and the prophets, read about astrology and other such like things, which are of slight (i) worth because they avail not for salvation, but lead to error ; and whoever devotes himself to these has no care for his soul ; while he who knows Christ finds a treasure house of wisdom and knowledge, because he knows that which is of avail.

Hence Bede says in the Book of Kings :

The clergy should not be prevented from reading profane literature. [*]

He harms the mental acumen of readers, and causes it to wane, who thinks that they should in every way be prevented from reading profane books ; for whatever useful things (k) are found in them it is lawful to adopt as one's own. Otherwise Moses and Daniel would not have been allowed to become learnèd in the wisdom and literature of the Egyptians and (*h*) I. e. Ethics, natural philosophy, rational philosophy.

(*i*) Compared with other knowledge. John.

* Summary. Certain men forbade Christians to read the books of the gentiles but Bede blames them, saying that they can well be read without sin because profit may be derived from them, as in the cases of Moses and Daniel, and also of Paul, who incorporated in his Epistles verses of the poets, e. g. " The Cretans &c. &c."

(*k*) He argues that the useful is not vitiated by the useless as XVII. q. IV. questi s. dist. IX. si ad scripturas. Contra Joan.

Chaldeans, whose superstitions and wantonness nevertheless they shuddered at.   And the teacher (*l*) of the gentiles himself would not have introduced (*m*) some verses of the poets into his own writings or sayings.

[On this Gratiàn comments :]

Then why * are those [writings] forbidden to be read which, it (*l*) For we read that when Paul had come to Athens he saw an altar of the Unknown God on which it was written : " This is an altar of (*b*) the Unknown God in whom we live and move and have our being." And with this inscription the Apostle began his exhortation and made known to those Athenians the meaning of this inscription, — continuing about our God and saying : " Whom you pronounce Unknown, Him declare I unto you and worship." Then Dionysius, the Areopagite, seeing a blind man passing by said to him (i. e. Paul), " If you will give sight to that blind man I will believe you." Immediately, when the name of Christ had been invoked, he was restored to sight and Dionysius believed.

(*m*) E. g. In the Epistle of Paul to Titus, the quotation from Epimenides the poet : " The Cretians are always liars, evil beasts, slow bellies." I. quaest. i. dominus declaravit.

Also he introduced in the first Epistle to the Corinthians this from Menander : " Evil communications often corrupt good manners." XXVIII. quaestio I. saepe.

He used also this verse : " I shall hate if I can : if not, I shall love against my will." But Jerome in his fifth division on Consecration often used verses from Virgil and Augustine, this of Lucan's : " Mens hausti nulla " &c. XXVI. quaestio V. nec mirum. And, as a lawyer, he uses the authority of Vergil. ff. de rerum divisione, intantrum § cenotaphium ; and also, of Homer, insti. de contrahen. emp. § pretium.

* Summary. Gratian solves the contradiction by saying that one ought to learn profane knowledge in addition, not for pleasure but for instruction, in order that the useful things, found therein may be turned to the use of sacred learning. Hence Gregory blamed a certain bishop, not for acquiring profane knowledge but because, for his pleasure, he expounded grammar instead of the Gospel.

(*b*) Another reading to the Unknown God, i. e. dative case.

Dionysius was converted by the preaching of Paul.

The Apostle used sentences from the poets.

is shown so reasonably, should be read? Some (*n*) read profane literature for their pleasure, being delighted with the productions of the poets and the charm of their words; while others learn them to add to their knowledge, in order that through reading the errors. of the heathen they may denounce them, and that they may turn to the service of sacred and devout learning the useful things they find therein. Such are praiseworthy in adding to their learning profane literature. Whence blessèd Gregory did not blame a certain bishop for learning it but because, contrary to his episcopal obligation, he read grammar to the people in place of the Gospel lesson.

Hence also Ambrose writes concerning Luke:

Profane writings should be read that they may not be unknown.

Some we read (*o*) that we may not neglect (*a*) them; we read that we may not be ignorant of them; we read not that we may embrace them but that we may reject them. (*b*)

So Jerome on the Epistle to Titus:

Grammar should be read in order that through it the Sacred Scriptures may be understood.

If anyone * has learned grammar or dialectics in order to have the ability to speak correctly and to discriminate between the true and the false, we do not blame them. Geometry (*c*) and Arithmetic and Music contain truth in their own range of knowledge, but that knowledge is not the knowledge of piety. The knowledge of piety is, — to know the law, to understand the prophets, to believe the Gospel, (and) not to be ignorant of the Apostles. Moreover the teaching of the grammarians can contribute to life, provided it has been applied to its higher uses.

Idem:

From the example of Daniel it is established that it is not a sin to be learned in profane literature. *

(*n*) Whence Saint Gregory in his LXXXVI Division, and in many places.

(*o*) This entire section should be read with regard to profane knowledge according to Jerome, and the threefold reason why it should be acquired is shown : namely that it be not neglected, that it be not unknown, that it may be refuted. So we read some, as the Old and New Testament, that we may not neglect them. Some we read (as the Arts) that we may not be ignorant of them. Some, as the writings of the heretics, that we may refute them. Some (we read) that they be not neglected, as the Old Testament.

Dan. I.

(*a*) For although of no use yet knowledge of them is necessary, as in dist. VII. cap. ult.

(*b*) As the books of heretics. As XXIV. quaestio III. cap. ult.

* Summary. This section is divided into two parts. In the first part it is set down that it is not blameworthy if one learns grammar and logic in order to distinguish the true and the false. In the second part which begins with " Geometry and Arithmetic " it is set down that the knowledges of the quadrivium have a truth of their own. But they are not the knowledges of piety, and are not to be so applied. But the Old and the New Testaments are knowledges of piety, and are to be applied. And grammar, if applied to good uses may be made profitable.

(*c*) Geometry. He does not mention Astronomy because this subject has fallen into disuse as XXVJ. quaest. II. § his ita.

* Summary. Two questions were propounded by Jerome. The first was whether it is a sin to learn the learning and knowledge of the pagans, and Jerome answers that it is not, and proves this by the example of four youths, Daniel, Ananias, Azarias, Misael, and by the example of Moses. For these, had they known it to be a sin would not have acquired the learning. For they did so in order to convince unbelievers. Otherwise

Those who are unwilling to partake of the table (*d*) [i. e. meat] and wine of the king, that they may not be defiled, surely would never consent to learn that which was unlawful if they knew that (*e*) the wisdom and learning of the Babylonians was sinful. They learn, however, not that they may conform thereto, but that they may judge and convict. For example, if any one ignorant of mathematics should wish to write against the mathematicians, he would expose himself to ridicule ; also in contending against the philosophers, if he should be ignorant of the dogmas of the philosophers. With this intent therefore they would learn the wisdom of the Chaldeans just as Moses had learned all the wisdom of the Egyptians. So too : If ever we are compelled to call to mind profane literature, and from it to learn things we before had omitted, it is not a matter of our personal desire, but, so to speak, of the weightiest necessity, — in order that we may prove that those events which were foretold (*f*) many ages ago by the holy prophets are contained (*g*) in the writings of the Greeks, as well as in those of the Latins and other Gentiles.

So, too, from the synod of Pope Eugene :

Bishops should appoint teachers and instructors in suitable places.[*]

The report has come to us with regard to certain regions that neither teachers, nor care for the pursuit of letters, is found. Therefore, in every way, care and diligence should be used by all the bishops among the peoples subject to them, and in other places where the necessity may arise, that teachers and instructors be appointed to teach assiduously the pursuit of letters and the principles of the liberal arts, because in them especially are the divine commands revealed and declared.

Likewise Augustine in his book against the Manichaeans :

The vanity of the gentiles is repressed and refuted by the use of their own authorities.

If the Sibyl or Orpheus or other soothsayers of the gentiles, they would have been exposed to ridicule if, when they were disputing with these unbelievers about their dogmas, they were found to know nothing about them. The second question was, whether it is a sin to cite secular laws in preaching or in discussion. And he replies that it is not, because it is necessary to prove that those things which the sacred writers have said are contained in the books of the heathen.

(*d*) Daniel, Ananias, Misael, Azarias. (*a*) For it is disgraceful for one who is in a discussion not to know the law in question.

(*e*) From the fact that Jerome here quotes the example of Daniel, the argument is derived that in doubtful cases recourse should be had to the example of our forefathers and others. XVI. quaest. I. sunt nonnulli. XXII. quaest. I. ut noveritis. I quaest. VII. convenientibus. XII. quaest. II questa. XVI. quaest. III. praesulum. XVI. quaest. I. cap. ult. XXVI. quaest. II. non statutum. et cap, non examplo. C. de sen. et interlo. nemo (*b*) contra. The solution is that where rules fail recourse must be had from similars to similars, otherwise not. XX. distinct. de quibus ; assuming that it is as there stated. Likewise the argument holds that good is assumed from the very fact that it has come from something good. As VII. quaest. I. omnis qui. & XXXIIII. quaest. I. cum beatissimus. IX. quaest. II. Lugdunensis. XII. quaest. I. expedit. XXVIII. quaest. I. sic enim. XXXI distinct. omnino. John.

(*f*) For example, as to the Incarnation, that passage in Virgil : " Jam nova progenies caelo demittitur ab alto."

(*g*) As that passage from Ovid, " Odero si potero : si non, invitus amabo."

* Summary. It was reported to Eugene at his Synod that in certain regions there were no teachers to instruct others in the liberal arts, and therefore he enjoined it upon all the bishops to establish teachers in suitable places to teach others daily in liberal doctrines.

[The notes on the remaining paragraphs of the text are here omitted owing to their length.]

Daniel and his companions.

(*a*) These were called under other names, Balthasar, Sidrac, Misac, and Abednago. According to Hugo and Lau.

(*b*) as for example XX dist. ca. fina.

Recourse is had at times from similars to similars.

Virgil.

Ovid.

or philosophers, are said to have foretold any truth, it certainly has weight in overcoming the vanity of the pagans; not, however, in leading to the acceptance of their authority. For as great as is the difference between the prediction of the coming of Christ by the angels and the confession of the devils, so great a difference is there between the authority of the prophets and the curiosity of the sacrilegious.

Likewise Pope Clement:

For the understanding of Sacred Scriptures knowledge of profane writings is shown to be necessary.

It has been reported to us that certain ones dwelling in your parts are opposed to the sacred teaching, and seem to teach just as it seems best to them, not according to the tradition of the fathers, but after their own understanding; for, as we have heard, certain ingenious men of your parts draw many analogies of the truth from the books they read. And there special care must be taken that when the law of God is read, it be not read or taught according to the individual's own mental ability and intelligence. For there are many words in divine scripture which can be drawn into that meaning which each one, of his own will, may assume for himself; but this should not be so, for you ought not to seek out a meaning that is external, foreign, and strange, in order, by any means whatsoever, to establish your view from the authority of scriptures; but you should derive from the scriptures themselves the meaning of the truth. And therefore it is fitting to gain knowledge of the scriptures from him who guards it according to the truth handed down to him by the fathers, and that he may be able correctly to impart that which he rightly learned. For when each one has learned from divine scriptures a sound and firm rule of truth, it will not be strange if from the common culture and liberal studies, which perhaps he touched upon in his youth, he should also bring something to the support of true doctrine, — in such manner, however, that when he learns the truth, he rejects the false and the feigned.

Likewise Isidorus in his book of Maxims:

Why Christians should be forbidden read the productions of the poets.

Christians are forbidden to read the productions of the poets because through the allurements of their fables the mind is too much stimulated toward the incentives to unlawful desires.

For not only by the offering of incense is sacrifice made to devils, but also by accepting too readily their sayings.

[Gratian draws the CONCLUSION.]

As therefore is evident from the authorities already quoted ignorance ought to be odious to priests. Since, if in ignorance of their own blindness they undertake to lead others, both fall into the ditch. Wherefore in the Psalm it is said: "Let their eyes be darkened that they may not see, and bow down their back always." For when those who go ahead are darkened, they who follow are easily inclined to bear the burdens of sinners. Therefore priests must endeavor to cast off ignorance from them as if it were a sort of pestilence. For although, in a few instances, it is said that a slave is flogged who does not do his master's will through ignorance of that will, this is not, generally understood of all. For the Apostle says: "If any man be ignorant, let him be ignorant," which is to be understood as referring to him who did not wish to have knowledge that he might do well.

Hence Augustine in his book of Questions:

Not every man who is ignorant is free from the penalty. For the ignorant man who is ignorant because he found no way of learning (the law) can be excused from the penalty, while he cannot be pardoned who having the means of knowledge did not use them.[1]

---

[1] *Decretum Gratiani, Distinctio* XXXVII. ed. Lyons, 1580.

(d) *Theology*

As above noted, one of the two great contributions of
the twelfth-century revival of learning to the field of
university studies was scholastic theology. The number
of books written on this subject was enormous. The
ponderous tomes, loaded with comments, make a long
array on the shelves of our great libraries, but they are
memorials of a battlefield of the mind now for the most
part deserted. The importance of the subject in the
scheme of mediaeval education has been much exag-
gerated; it was the pursuit of a very small minority of
students. It has a certain interest to the historian of
education, however, as an illustration of the way in which
a method struck out by a single original thinker may
influence the work of scholars and universities for generations. The method of scholastic theology is mainly
due to Abelard.

The roots of the nobly developed systems of the thirteenth
century theology lie in the twelfth century; and all Sums of
Theology, of which there was a considerable number, not only
before Alexander of Hales [thirteenth century] but also before
and at the time of Peter Lombard, may be traced back directly
or indirectly to Paris.[1]

In this mass of theological writings one book stands
out as the contribution which for three centuries most
influenced university instruction in theology. This is the
"Sentences" (*Sententiae*) of Peter Lombard (c. 1100–1160),
in four books. The subjects discussed in this work are
similar to those treated by Abelard in the *Sic et Non*

[1] Denifle, I, 46.

(see p. 20). In not a few instances it adopts the form of presentation used in that book, i. e., the citation of authorities on both sides of the case. Like the *Decretum* of Gratian, it is an illustration of the widespread influence of the *Sic et Non*.

A great number of commentaries were written upon this book. A manuscript note in one of the copies in the Harvard library states that four hundred and sixty such commentaries are known; but I have been unable to verify the statement.

In theory, the Bible was studied in the Faculties of Theology in addition to the " Sentences "; but in the thirteenth century and later it seems to have occupied, in practice, a minor share of the student's attention. To this effect is the criticism of Roger Bacon in 1292:

Although the principal study of the theologian ought to be in the text of Scripture, as I have proved in the former part of this work, yet in the last fifty years theologians have been principally occupied with questions [for debate] as all know, in tractates and summae, — horse-loads, composed by many, — and not at all with the most holy text of God. And accordingly, theologians give a readier reception to a treatise of scholastic questions than they will do to one about the text of Scripture. . . . The greater part of these questions introduced into theology, with all the modes of disputation (see p. 115) and solution, are in the terms of philosophy, as is known to all theologians, who have been well exercised in philosophy before proceeding to theology. Again, other questions which are in use among theologians, though in terms of theology, viz., of the Trinity, of the fall, of the incarnation, of sin, of virtue, of the sacraments, etc., are mainly ventilated by authorities, arguments, and solutions drawn from philosophy. And therefore the entire occupation of theologians now-a-days is philosophical, both in substance and method.[1]

(e) *Medicine*

The medical learning of western Europe was greatly enlarged during the eleventh and twelfth centuries by the translation into Latin of numerous works by Greek, Arabic, and Jewish physicians. These became the stand-ard text-books of the Faculties or Schools of Medicine. The Greek writers most commonly mentioned in the university lists of studies are Hippocrates (fifth century B. C.) and Galen (second century A. D.). Several of their more important works were first translated — like those of Aristotle — from Arabic versions of the original Greek. Avicenna (c. 980–1037) furnished the most important Arabic contribution. Accounts of these men and their writings may be found in any good encyclopedia. For the program of studies at Paris see D. C. Munro, " Trans-lations and Reprints," Vol. II, Pt. III. A list of the books used at Montpellier, one of the most important medical schools, is given in Rashdall, Vol. II, Pt. I, p. 123, and Pt. II, p. 780; the list for Oxford, p. 454 f.

(f) *Other University Text-books*

The foregoing sections indicate the books which fur-nished the intellectual basis for the rise of universities, and particularly the basis for their division into Facul-ties. They do not indicate by any means the whole list of books used in the universities between 1200 and 1500; nor is it possible here to give such a list. Two

[1] *Compendium Studii Theologiae;* translated by J. S. Brewer in R. Bacon, *Opera Inedita*, p. lvi.

facts only are to be noted concerning them: First, a considerable number of books already well known in the twelfth century were used in addition to those mentioned above. Among these may be mentioned the Latin grammars of Donatus (*fl.* 350 A. D.) and Priscian (*fl.* 500 A. D.), treatises by Boethius (*c.* 475–525) on Rhetoric, Logic, Arithmetic, and Music, and his translations of various portions of the *Organon* of Aristotle, and of the *Isagoge*, or Introduction to the Categories of Aristotle, by Porphyry (*c.* 233–306). The Geometry of Euclid (*fl.* 300 B. C.) was translated about 1120 by Adelard of Bath, and the Astronomy (Almagest) of Ptolemy (second century A. D.) was pharaphrased from the Arabic by Gerard of Cremona toward the close of the twelfth century, under the title *Theorica Planetarum.*

Second, during the whole period under discussion there was an active production of new text-books on the established subjects, some of which were widely used in the universities. Among the grammars was the *Doctrinale* of Alexander da Villa Dei, written in 1199. This rhyming grammar was enormously popular, and continued to be so, well into the sixteenth century. The *Grecismus* and *Labyrinthus* of Eberhard of Bcthune (early thirteenth century), also grammars in rhyme, were widely used. Logical treatises often mentioned in university programs of study were *De Sex Principiis* (On the Six Principles), written about 1150 by Gilbert de la Porrée, a teacher of John of Salisbury; and the *Summulae* of Petrus Hispanus (thirteenth century). In the thirteenth century Albertus Magnus made a digest of all the works of Aristotle, which proved to be easier for students than the originals, and which were sometimes used in place of them. Among mathematical works of this century were the *Algorismus* (Arithmetic) and the *Libellus de Sphaera* (On the Sphere) by John Holywood (Sacrobosco ;) and the *Perspectiva Communis*, i. e. Optics, by John (Peckham) of Pisa. A treatise on Music by John de Muris of Paris was produced in the early part of the fourteenth century. All of these were well-known university text-books. They appear in the list at Leipzig throughout the fifteenth century (see p. 139).

4. PRIVILEGES

The privileges granted by civil and ecclesiastical powers constitute a fourth important influence upon the growth of universities. Beginning with the year 1158 a long series of immunities, liberties, and exemptions was bestowed by State and Church upon masters and students as a class, and upon universities as corporations. Masters and scholars were, for example, often taken under the special protection of the sovereign of the country in which they were studying; they were exempted from taxation, and from military service; most important of all, they were placed under the jurisdiction of special courts, in which alone they could be tried. Universities as corporations were given, among other privileges, the right to confer upon their graduates the license to teach " anywhere in the world " without further examination, and the very important right to suspend lectures, i. e. to strike, pending the settlement of grievances against State or Church. They had, of course, the general legal powers of corporations. Thus fortified, the universities attained an astonishing degree of independence and power; and their members were enabled to live in unusual liberty and security. This fact in itself unquestionably tended to increase the university population.

The masters and scholars of Bologna, Paris, and Oxford seem to have led the way in securing privileges. Their precedent made it easier for later universities to secure similar rights. These were sometimes established "with all the privileges of Paris and Bologna," or "all the privileges of any other university."

The authorities who granted privileges were the sovereigns of various countries, — the Emperor of the Holy Roman Empire, the kings of France, England, the Spains — feudal lords, municipalities, and the Pope or his legates. They usually conferred them upon special universities, or upon the masters and students in specified towns, and sometimes only for a definite term of years. Minor privileges differed greatly in different localities, but the more important ones — indicated above — were possessed by nearly all universities.

The documents which follow illustrate both the variety of privileges and the variety of authorities who granted them.

(a) *Special Protection is granted by the Sovereign*

1. The earliest known privilege of any kind connected with the history of mediaeval universities is the *Authentic Habita*. It was granted by Frederick Barbarossa (Frederick I), Emperor of the Holy Roman Empire, at the Diet of Roncaglia, Italy, in 1158; probably

through the influence of Doctors of Law from Bologna. These men were doubtless familiar with the fact that similar privileges had been given to teachers and scholars by various Roman emperors, some of which were preserved in the Code of Justinian (see p. 54). The *Authentic Habita* may be regarded as the revival of an ancient Roman custom. The section of the *Authentic* granting the special protection of the Emperor follows:

After careful inquiry of the bishops, abbots, dukes, counts, judges, and other nobles of our sacred palace in regard to this matter, we, in our loving-kindness, do grant to all scholars who are travelling for the sake of study, and especially to professors of divine and sacred laws, this privilege: Both they and their messengers are to come in security to the places in which the studies are carried on, and there they are to abide in security. For we think it proper, in order that they may be upheld in their good works by our fame and protection, to defend from all harm, by definite special favor, those by whose knowledge the world is illumined unto obedience to God and to us his servants, and the lives of our subjects are moulded. . . . Therefore by this law, which is of general effect, and is to be valid forever, we decree that hereafter no one shall show himself so bold as to presume to inflict any injury upon scholars, or, for an offence committed in their former province, to impose any fine upon them, — which, we have heard, sometimes happens through an evil custom. And let violators of this decree, and the local rulers at the time in case they have themselves neglected to punish such violation, know surely that a four-fold restitution of property shall be exacted from all, and that in addition to the brand of infamy affixed to them by the law itself, they shall be forever deprived of their official positions.[1]

[1] One sentence of no importance is omitted from the translation. The rest of the document is given below, p. 90. For a slightly different version see D. C. Munro, "Translations and Reprints from the Original Sources of European History," Vol. II, Pt. III, p. 2.

2. In 1200 Philip Augustus of France made certain regulations regarding the protection of students at Paris, and entrusted their execution to the Provost of that city. This is the earliest known charter of privileges for Paris.   It should be read in connection with the following selection.   For the text in full see D. C. Munro, *l. c.* p. 4.

Small causes, great events!   As is narrated in the contemporary account given below, a simple tavern brawl led to the granting of these extensive privileges. This is one among many examples of the way in which the universities turned similar events to their own advantage.   The passage also exhibits a typical conflict between town and gown.

On the dissension which existed between the Scholars and the Citizens of Paris.   [1200 A. D.]

In that same year a grave dissension arose between the scholars and the citizens of Paris, the origin of which was as follows:

There was at Paris a notable German scholar who was bishop-elect of Liége.   His servant, while buying wine at a tavern, was beaten and his wine jar was broken.   When this was known, the German clerks came together and entering the tavern they wounded the host, and having beaten him they went off, leaving him half dead.   Therefore there was an outcry among the people and the city was stirred, so that Thomas, the Provost of Paris, under arms, and with an armed mob of citizens, broke into the Hall of the German clerks, and in their combat that notable scholar who was bishop-elect of Liége, was killed, with some of his people.

Therefore the Masters of the scholars in Paris going to the King of France complained to him of Thomas, the Provost of Paris and of his accomplices who killed the aforesaid scholars.

And at their instance the aforesaid Thomas was arrested, as were certain of his accomplices, and put in prison.   But some of them escaped by flight, leaving their homes and occupations ; then the King of France, in his wrath, had their houses demolished and their vines and fruit trees uprooted.

But as to the Provost, it was decided that he should be kept in prison, not to be released until he should clear himself by the ordeal of water or sword, and if he failed, he should be hung, and if he was cleared he should, by the King's clemency, leave the kingdom.

And yet the scholars, pitying him, entreated the King of France that the Provost and his accomplices after being flogged after the manner of scholars at school, should be let alone and be restored to their occupations.

But the King of France would not grant this, saying that it would be greatly derogatory to his honor if any one but himself should punish his malefactors.   Furthermore, this same King of France, being afraid that the Masters of the scholars, and the scholars themselves, would withdraw from his city, sought to satisfy them by decreeing that for the future no clerk should be haled to a secular trial on account of any misdemeanor which he had committed, but that if the clerk committed a misdemeanor he should be delivered over to the Bishop and be dealt with in accordance with the clerk's court.   Also this same King of France decreed that whoever was the Provost of Paris should take oath that he would be loyal to the clerks, saving his loyalty to the King.   Moreover this same King conferred upon the scholars his own sure peace and confirmed it to them by his own charter.

But that Provost, when he had been detained in the King's prison for many days planned his escape by flight, and, as he was being lowered over the wall, the rope broke, and falling from a height to the ground, he was killed.[1]

[1] Roger de Hoveden, *Chronica*, ed. Stubbs, IV, 120, 121.

3. Special protection for a limited time is granted more explicitly by Philip IV in 1306:

Philip, by the grace of God King of France and Navarre, to our Provost at Paris, greeting. Whereas the University, masters and Scholars at Paris, are under our special guardianship and protection as they — both Masters, and Scholars as well — come to their studies, stay in the said city, or return to their own places ; and inasmuch as injuries, annoyances, oppression, and violence are frequently inflicted upon them, as we have heard, not only in your prefecture but in other places also, to the prejudice of our guardianship, — which wrongs could not be prosecuted outside of Paris in any way which would prevent them from being distracted from their studies, to their serious prejudice and that of the aforesaid University, and from being harassed by serious struggles and expense, — therefore we entrust and commit to you their protection and custody, and in addition thereto the restraint of those persons who, to the prejudice of our protection and guardianship, inflict upon the above-mentioned Masters or Scholars unjust violence, injury or loss, either within the limits of your prefecture or in other places of our kingdom, wheresoever the aforesaid wrongs are committed.

This present arrangement is to be in force for a period of two years only.[1]

4. The personal property of Masters and Scholars is protected.

The privilege of Philip Augustus for Paris, 1200.

Also our judges [of the secular courts] shall not lay hands on the chattels of the students at Paris for any crime whatever. But if it seem that these ought to be sequestrated, they shall be sequestrated and guarded after sequestration by the ecclesias-

---

[1] *Chart. Univ. Paris.*, Vol. II, No. 657.

tical judge, in order that whatever is judged legal by the ecclesiastical judge may be done.[1]

More comprehensive protection is given by the charter of Philip IV, 1340/41, concerning Masters and Scholars at Paris. The king decrees —

Likewise, that their goods and means of support, whereon they have and will have to live in pursuing their studies as aforesaid, in consideration of their status, shall not be taken for our use or that of our subjects or be in any way whatever interfered with under cover of wars or any other pretext whatever, by any persons whatever, of whatever condition, status, or prominence they may be.[2]

(b) *The Sovereign grants to Scholars the Right of Trial in Special Courts, in the City in which they are studying*

This remarkable privilege was one great source of the liberty of mediaeval scholars. Under its protection they could not be summoned to a court outside the university town, even to answer for an offense committed elsewhere; the plaintiff must appear at the town in which they were studying, and before specified judges, who were at least not inclined to deal severely with scholars. At Paris scholars were not only protected as defendants, but they had the right as plaintiffs to summon the accused to Paris.

1. The earliest document on the subject is the concluding section of the *Authentic Habita*, described above:

Moreover, should anyone presume to bring a lawsuit against the scholars on any ground, the choice [of judges] in the mat-

[1] Quoted from D. C. Munro, *Translations and Reprints*, Vol. II, Pt. III.

[2] *Chart. Univ. Paris.*, II, No. 1044.

ter shall be given to the said scholars, who may meet their accusers before either their professors or the bishop of the city, to whom we have given jurisdiction in this matter.   But if, in sooth, the accusers shall attempt to hale the scholar before another judge, the scholar shall escape from the merited punishment, even though the cause be most just, because of such attempt.

This provision is reminiscent of, if not actually inspired by, a similar provision for scholars in the Code of Justinian (see p. 54). The *Authentic Habita* as a whole is important as the fundamental charter of university privileges in Italy, if not in other countries.   It was not granted to a university, — indeed, no university was apparently then in existence, — nor to the scholars of any special town; it was " of general effect."   But " this pre-university charter was usually recognized as the basis of all the special privileges conferred on particular (Italian) universities by the States in which they were situated." [1]   Probably it suggested, directly or indirectly, the granting of similar privileges to universities in other countries.   It certainly affected those universities which were founded " with all the privileges of any other university."   Two further illustrations follow.

2. In 1245 Pope Innocent IV exempted students at Paris from citation to ecclesiastical courts outside of Paris, in order that their studies might not be interrupted :

To the masters and scholars at Paris.   In order that you may carry on your studies more freely and be less occupied with other business, we grant your petitions, and by the author-

1 Rashdall, I, p. 147.

ity of this present letter bestow upon you the privilege of not being haled by apostolic letters beyond the limits of the city of Paris upon questions that have arisen within its limits, unless [these letters] make express mention of this privilege.[1]

3. The same privilege was granted as regards civil courts by Philip IV in 1340/41 :

. . . The Masters and Scholars studying at Paris, if summoned by any secular judges of our realm, shall not be haled and cited to their courts outside of Paris ; nor shall laymen who are subject to our rule attempt to bring this about.[2]

This right was known at Paris as the *jus non trahi extra* (right of not being haled outside). " It became henceforth *the* characteristic university privilege, not only of Paris but of all universities which were in any degree influenced by Parisian usage." [3]

(c) *Exemption from Taxation*

One of the most important privileges enjoyed by modern universities (in common with other educational institutions, and with churches) is exemption from taxation. This privilege is directly traceable to those of the mediaeval universities, and possibly through them to Roman laws on the subject. In the early history of universities the privilege was held, not by the corporations as such, but by masters and scholars as individuals.

1. One example of such exemption is found in the charter of Philip IV, 1340/41, already quoted:

[1] *Chart. Univ. Paris.*, I, No. 142.
[2] *l. c.*, II, No. 1044.   [3] Rashdall, I, p. 343.

To the aforesaid Masters and Scholars [of Paris], now in attendance at the University, and to those who are hereafter to come to the same University, or who are actually preparing in sincerity so to come, also while [they are] staying at the University, or returning to their own homes, *we grant*. . . that no layman, of whatever condition or prominence he may be, whether he be a private person, prefect, or bailiff, shall disturb, molest, or presume otherwise in any way whatsoever to seek to extort anything from the aforesaid Masters and Scholars, in person, family or property, under pretext of toll, *tallia* [special form of feudal tax], tax, customs, or other such personal taxes, or other personal exaction of any kind, while they are either coming to the University itself, or actually preparing in sincerity to come, or returning to their own homes ; and whose status as scholars shall be established by the proper oath.

2. The charter of the University of Leipzig, in 1409, exempts certain property of the corporation, as such, from taxes :

Likewise in said town, in behalf of the aforesaid University, and for the increase of the same, we have instituted and founded two Colleges, . . . and for these we have given and assigned two houses . . . and these same houses of the said Colleges we have made free from all *losunge*, exactions, contributions, *steura*, laws, taxes, and from the control of the citizens of the beforementioned town ; and of our sure knowledge we incorporate them and make them free for the advantage of the aforesaid University.[1]

The words *steura* and *losunge* refer to special forms of taxes whose exact nature is not known.

3. Not only were Masters, students, and corporate property exempt from taxation, but also persons connected with the universities in subordinate capacities.

[1] F. Zarncke, *Statutenbücher der Universität Leipzig*, p. 4.

There was much dispute in some places as to the number and occupations of those who might be thus exempted. The following letter of Henry VI of England to the University of Caen, Normandy, settles one of these disputes.

On January 22, 1450, the King refused to free the dependents of the university from taxation. The Masters and Scholars thereupon made formal complaint to him that this refusal hindered the free and peaceful pursuit of their studies as guaranteed by his charter of 1432 (see p. 103). In reply (February 13, 1450), the King recognized the justice of the complaint and granted the desired privilege. Compare the similar exemption in the Harvard Charter of 1650 (p. 101). The letter is apparently addressed to the Bailiff of Caen and other royal officials.

Nevertheless since those letters of ours [of January 22] were sent, proper and true objection has been made to us as to those privileges, whereby we have well understood that the Doctors, Masters, Scholars, dependents, officers, households and servitors should not be subject to or obliged to contribute to such villein-taxes, aides, and octrois.

Therefore is it, that we — wishing our letters, gifts of privileges, and commands to be guarded and supported without any diminution or loss in any manner whatever, but to be increased, augmented and maintained — have regarded and also considered the fact that said members of our said daughter [i. e. the University] could not well carry out the requirements of study, or continue therein, if their servitors and households did not enjoy and use such and similar privileges as said members. Desiring, with all our heart the maintenance, continuation and increase of our said University which (not without good reason) we have under our special favor, considering these things, with the advice and counsel of our very dear and very beloved Cousin Edmond, Duke of Somerset, Lieutenant-General and Governor in our stead of our realms of France, the country and Duchy of Normandy, we command and strictly enjoin you all and each one of you so far as he shall be concerned, that you make or cause to be made free and exempt from said villein-taxes, aides, and octrois, one advocate, one purveyor, one bell-ringer, two booksellers, two parchment makers, two illuminators, two bookbinders, six beadles, five bailiffs, (one for each of the five Faculties) and seven messengers (understanding that there shall be one for each diocese in our said Duchy), and this you shall do up to this number of attendants and servitors of this our University, and at the same time, uphold, maintain and continue them in their rights, franchises, and liberties, of which by our said command, foundation, and augmentation, you find them to be and to have been duly possessed, without suffering anything to disturb or interfere with this.

And, although in our other letters devoted to the regulation of this University the said five bailiffs and seven messengers were not in any way included, yet by special grace through these present letters, to the end that our said University may be able to have the servitors necessary to it, without whom the requirements of study could not be continued and maintained, we wish the said five bailiffs and seven messengers to enjoy such and similar privileges as the rest who are named in our other said letters of regulation, notwithstanding that the said letters and any others whatever may require, or seem to require, the contrary to this.

And that the aforesaid suppliants may be able to have, at their need, these present letters in various and diverse places, we wish that copies of these, made under the royal seal, be in good faith made like the original.[1]

[1] Fournier, *Statuts et Priv. des Univ. franç.*, III, No. 1673.

(d) *The Privilege of suspending Lectures* (Cessatio)

One of the most effective privileges of mediaeval universities was the right of suspending lectures. This was used again and again in cases of unredressed grievances against civil or ecclesiastical authorities, — more particularly against the former. A *cessatio* was usually followed by a migration of masters and scholars to some other university, unless satisfaction was promptly forthcoming. Such a migration was a serious blow to the commercial prosperity of any town; consequently the "cessation" was an instrument of great power for the extraction of all sorts of local concessions. It was often exercised without express authorization by civil or ecclesiastical powers, but the privilege was distinctly conferred by a bull of Pope Gregory IX for Paris in 1231:

And if, perchance, the assessment [right to fix the prices] of lodgings is taken from you, or anything else is lacking, or an injury or outrageous damage, such as death or the mutilation of a limb, is inflicted on one of you, unless through a suitable admonition satisfaction is rendered within fifteen days, you may suspend your lectures until you have received full satisfaction. And if it happens that any one of you is unlawfully imprisoned, unless the injury ceases on a remonstrance from you, you may, if you judge it expedient, suspend your lectures immediately.[1]

The events leading up to the granting of this privilege are worth recounting as an illustration of the way in which such rights were frequently secured. The "clerks" referred to were of course scholars. The cessation of

[1] *Chart. Univ. Paris.*, Vol. I, p. 59. Quoted from D. C. Munro, *l. c.* p. 9.

lectures was followed by a migration to other cities until satisfaction was given. The exact nature of the satisfaction given by the king is not known. One important result, however, was the great charter of papal privileges just referred to, — " the *Magna Charta* of the University" of Paris.[1]

" Concerning the discord that arose at Paris between the whole body of clergy and the citizens, and concerning the withdrawal of the clergy" [1229]:

In that same year, on the second and third holidays before Ash Wednesday, days when the clerks of the university have leisure for games, certain of the clerks went out of the City of Paris in the direction of Saint Marcel's, for a change of air and to have contests in their usual games. When they had reached the place and had amused themselves for some time in carrying on their games, they chanced to find in a certain tavern some excellent wine, pleasant to drink. And then, in the dispute that arose between the clerks who were drinking and the shop keepers, they began to exchange blows and to tear each other's hair, until some townsmen ran in and freed the shop keepers from the hands of the clerks ; but when the clerks resisted they inflicted blows upon them and put them to flight, well and thoroughly pommelled. The latter, however, when they came back much battered into the city, roused their comrades to avenge them. So on the next day they came with swords and clubs to Saint Marcel's, and entering forcibly the house of a certain shop keeper, broke up all his wine casks and poured the wine out on the floor of the house. And, proceeding through the open squares, they attacked sharply whatever man or woman they came upon and left them half dead from the blows given them.

But the Prior of Saint Marcel's, as soon as he learned of this great injury done to his men, whom he was bound to defend,

[1] For the text of this charter in full, see D. C. Munro, *l. c.* p. 7.

lodged a complaint with the Roman legate and the Bishop of Paris. And they went together in haste to the Queen, to whom the management of the realm had been committed at that time, and asked her to take measures for the punishment of such a wrong. But she, with a woman's forwardness, and impelled by mental excitement, immediately gave orders to the prefects of the city and to certain of her own ruffians [mercenary body-guard] with all speed to go out of the city, under arms, and to punish the authors of the violence, sparing no one. Now as these armed men, who were prone to act cruelly at every opportunity, left the gates of the city, they came upon a number of clerks busy just outside the city walls with games, — men who were entirely without fault in connection with the aforesaid violence, since those who had begun the riotous strife were men from the regions adjoining Flanders, whom we commonly call Picards. But, notwithstanding this, the police, rushing upon these men who they saw were unarmed and innocent, killed some, wounded others, and handled others mercilessly, battering them with the blows they inflicted on them. But some of them escaping by flight lay hid in dens and caverns. And among the wounded it was found that there were two clerks, rich and of great influence, who died, one of them being by race a man of Flanders, and the other of the Norman Nation.

But when the enormity of this transgression reached the ears of the Masters of the University they came together in the presence of the Queen and Legate, having first suspended entirely all lectures and debates, and strenuously demanded that justice be shown them for such a wrong. For it seemed to them disgraceful that so light an occasion as the transgression of certain contemptible little clerks should be taken to create prejudice against the whole university ; but let him who was to blame in the transgression be the one to suffer the penalty.

But when finally every sort of justice had been refused them by the King and the Legate, as well as by the Bishop, there took place a universal withdrawal of the Masters and a scattering of the Scholars, the instruction of the Masters and the training of the pupils coming to an end, so that not one person of note out of them all remained in the city. And the city which was wont to boast of her clerks now remained bereft of them. . . . Thus withdrawing, the clerks betook themselves practically in a body to the larger cities in various districts. But the largest part of them chose the metropolitan city of Angers for their university instruction. Thus, then, withdrawing from the City of Paris, the nurse of Philosophy and the foster mother of Wisdom, the clerks execrated the Roman Legate and cursed the womanish arrogance of the Queen, nay, also, their infamous unanimity [in the matter]. . . .

At length, through the efforts of discreet persons, it was worked out that, certain things being done to meet the situation as required by the faults on both sides, peace was made up between the clerks and citizens and the whole body of scholars was recalled.[1]

Not infrequently a university which had decreed a cessation was invited to establish itself elsewhere. The cessation at Paris in 1229 was followed by an urgent invitation from the King of England:

The King; Greeting to the Masters and the whole body of scholars at Paris. Humbly sympathizing with the exceeding tribulations and distresses which you have suffered at Paris under an unjust law, we wish by our pious aid, with reverence to God and His holy church, to restore your status to its proper condition of liberty. Wherefore we have concluded to make known to your entire body that if it shall be your pleasure to transfer yourselves to our kingdom of England and to remain there to study we will for this purpose assign to you cities, boroughs, towns, whatsoever you may wish to select, and in every fitting way will cause you to rejoice in a state of liberty and tranquillity which should please God and fully meet your needs.

[1] Matthew Paris, *Chronica Majora*, III, 166–169.

In testi.nony of which &c.   Witnessed by the King at Reading, July 16. [1229].[1]

(e) *The Right of Teaching everywhere* (Jus ubique docendi)

Masters and Doctors of the three leading universities, Paris, Bologna, and Oxford, were early recognized as qualified to teach anywhere without further examination, by virtue of the superior instruction given at those institutions.   Their degrees were in strictness merely licenses to teach within the dioceses in which they were granted. The recognition of these licenses elsewhere grew up as a matter of custom, not by any express authorization. At least one other university (Padua, founded 1222) acquired the privilege in the same way.   Later universities, — or the cities in which they were established, — desiring to gain equal prestige for their graduates, obtained from the Pope or from the Emperor of the Holy Roman Empire bulls conferring upon them the same privilege.   Even Paris and Bologna formally received it from the Pope in 1292.   "From this time the notion gradually gained ground that the *jus ubique docendi* was of the essence of a Studium Generale, and that no school which did not possess it could obtain it without a Bull from Emperor or Pope."   "It was usually but not quite invariably, conferred in express terms by the original foundation-bulls; and was apparently understood to be involved in the mere act of erection even in the rare cases where it is not expressly conceded." [2]   In prac-

---

[1] *Chart. Univ. Paris.*, I, p. 119.

[2] Rashdall, I, pp. 11, 12.

tice, the graduates of almost all universities where subject to further examination in one Studium or another before being admitted to teach there, although the graduates of the leading universities may have been very generally received without such test. The privilege is more important in officially marking the rank of a school as a Studium Generale, i. e. a place of higher education, in which instruction was given, by a considerable number of masters, in at least one of the Faculties of Arts, Theology, Law, and Medicine, and to which students were attracted, or at least invited, from all countries.

The Bull granting the *jus ubique docendi* to Paris (Pope Nicholas IV, 1292) is here printed, although it is not the earliest example; a similar Bull was issued for Toulouse as early as 1233. The rhetorical introduction is omitted, as in most instances above.

Desiring, therefore, that the students in the field of knowledge in the city of Paris, may be stimulated to strive for the reward of a Mastership, and may be able to instruct, in the Faculties in which they have deserved to be adorned with a Master's chair, all those who come from all sides, — we decree, by this present letter, that whoever of our University in the aforesaid city shall have been examined and approved by those through whom, under Apostolic authority, the right to lecture is customarily bestowed on licentiates in said faculties, according to the custom heretofore observed there, — and who shall have from them license in the Faculty of Theology, or Canon Law, or Medicine, or the Liberal Arts, — shall thenceforward have authority to teach everywhere outside of the aforesaid city, free from examination or test, either public or private, or any other new regulation as to lecturing or teaching. Nor shall he be prohibited by anyone, all other customs and statutes to the contrary notwithstanding ; and whether he wishes to lecture or not in the Faculties referred to, he shall nevertheless be regarded as a Doctor.[1]

(f) *Privileges granted by a Municipality*

Not infrequently mediaeval cities granted special privileges to universities and their members.   These cities recognized the commercial and other advantages resulting from the presence of a large body of students within their gates, and made substantial concessions to retain them, or to secure the settlement of a university which might be migrating from some other city.   Instances of the latter kind are numerous in the free cities of Italy.   These privileges included very ample legal jurisdiction by the Rector of the university in cases affecting scholars, payment of professors' salaries by the city, exemption from taxes, loans to scholars at a low rate of interest, and guarantees against extortionate prices for food and other necessaries.

1. The following examples are cited, among many others in the statutes of the city of Padua :

The town of Padua binds itself to make loans to scholars, according to the quality of the scholars, upon good and sufficient securities or bonds worth a third more than the loan, and upon the oath and promise of the scholars that they accept the loan on their own account and for their own use in meeting their personal expenses and not for any other person or persons or for the use of others.   (1260 A. D.)

Every six months the Chief Magistrate of Padua shall appoint two money lenders for the scholars, — judges or laymen at the will of the Rector of the scholars — who shall have charge of the town's money that is to be loaned to the scholars.   And

[1] *Chart. Univ. Paris.*, II, No. 578.

they shall, in the name of the town, make loans to the scholars in accordance with the statutes and the agreement of the scholars, and at their own risk' entirely, so that the town of Padua shall not incur loss. And the money lenders shall themselves deposit in the town treasury good and sufficient security as to this. (1268.)

Scholars shall be regarded as citizens with regard to matters advantageous, but not with regard to matters disadvantageous to them. (1261.)

Scholars shall not be required to pay the *tolloneum* (i. e. taxes on imports, collected at the city gates). (1262.) [1]

2. A generation preceding the date of these statutes a large part of the university, dissatisfied with its treatment at Padua, migrated to Vercelli, more than one hundred and fifty miles away. The contract (1228 A. D.) between the rectors of the university and the proctors representing the town contains numerous privileges, among which are the following:

Likewise the aforesaid proctors have promised in the name of the town of Vercelli that the town will loan to the scholars, and to the university of scholars, the sum of ten thousand pounds, papal money, at the rate of two pence for two years, and thereafter three pence for six years [under proper security. The customary rate seems to have been four pence.] . . . Likewise, when a scholar shall have paid the money loaned to him, the town of Vercelli will retain that amount in the common treasury as principal, and from it will help some other needy scholar under the same agreement and similar conditions. . . . Likewise, the town of Vercelli will not allow provisions within the town limits to be withdrawn from their markets [in order to raise the price?] but will cause them to be delivered in the city in good faith, and will cause them to be put on sale

[1] Documents printed by Denifle, *Die Universitäten*, etc., pp. 801–803.

twice a week. . . . [Also one thousand bushels of grain shall be put in the city granary and sold to scholars at cost in time of need.] . . . Likewise the town of Vercelli shall provide salaries [for professors] which shall be deemed competent by two scholars and two townsmen, and if they disagree the Bishop shall decide the matter. . . . and said salaries shall be for one Theologian, three Masters of Laws, two Decretists, two Decretalists, two teachers of Natural Philosophy, two Logicians, and two Grammarians. [These professors shall be chosen by the rectors of the university. The town will send out at its own expense] trustworthy messengers under oath, who shall in good faith, and in the interests of the university of Vercelli, seek out the chosen Masters and Teachers, and shall use their best endeavors to bind them to lecture in the city of Vercelli. [The town will preserve peace within its borders, will consider scholars and their messengers neutral in time of war, will grant them the rights of citizens, and will respect the legal jurisdiction of the rectors, except in criminal and other specially mentioned cases.]

Likewise, the town of Vercelli will prcvide two copyists, through whom it will undertake to furnish men able to supply to the scholars copies in both kinds of Law [Civil and Canon] and in Theology, which shall be satisfactory and accurate both in text and in glosses, and the students shall pay for their copies [no extortionate prices but] a rate based on the estimate of the rectors [of the university].

. . . Likewise, the scholars or their representatives shall not pay the tributes in the district of Vercelli which belong and accrue to the town of Vercelli. . . . The Podesta [Chief Magistrate] and the town itself shall be bound to send, throughout the cities of Italy and elsewhere, (as shall seem expedient to them) notice that a university has been established at Vercelli, and to invite scholars to come to the University of Vercelli.[1]

[1] Document printed by Rashdall, II, Pt. II, p. 746.

The whole contract was made a part of the city statutes and was to be in force for eight years.

(g) *The Influence of Mediaeval Privileges on Modern Universities.*

There is no question that the long series of privileges granted to mediaeval universities influences the university life of to-day. Out of many illustrations of this fact two are here cited as affecting American higher education. The reader will observe in these paragraphs from the charters of Harvard College and Brown University the familiar exemption of corporate property from taxation, and the exemption of persons connected with these institutions not only from taxes, but also from other public duties. The charter of Brown University refers explicitly to European university privileges. Both of these charters, with some amendments, are still in force.

And, further, be it ordered by this Court and the authority thereof, that all the lands, tenements, or hereditaments, houses, or revenues, within this jurisdiction, to the aforesaid President or College appertaining, not exceeding the value of five hundred pounds per annum, shall from henceforth be freed from all civil impositions, taxes, and rates ; all goods to the said Corporation, or to any scholars thereof, appertaining, shall be exempted from all manner of toll, customs, and excise whatsoever ; and that the said President, Fellows, and scholars, together with the servants, and other necessary officers to the said President or College appertaining, not exceeding ten, — viz. three to the President and seven to the College belonging, — shall be exempted from all personal civil offices, military exercises or services, watchings and wardings ; and such of their estates, not exceeding one hundred pounds a man, shall be free from all country taxes or rates whatsoever, and none others.[1]

And furthermore, for the greater encouragement of the Seminary of learning, and that the same may be amply endowed and enfranchised with the same privileges, dignities, and immunities enjoyed by the American colleges, and European universities, We do grant, enact, ordain, and declare, and it is hereby granted, enacted, ordained, and declared, That the College estate, the estates, persons, and families of the President and Professors, for the time being, lying, and being within the Colony, with the persons of the Tutors and students, during their residence at the College, shall be freed and exempted from all taxes, serving on juries, and menial services : And that the persons aforesaid shall be exempted from bearing arms, impresses, and military services, except in case of an invasion.[2]

Exemption from "watchings and wardings," and from "military services, except in case of an invasion," is not included in the list of privileges cited in the preceding sections, but it was often conferred on mediaeval universities in almost the exact terms of these charters.

5. The Initiative of Civil or Ecclesiastical Powers

Many universities originated without the express initiative of any civil or ecclesiastical power. They either grew up slowly, as in the cases of Bologna and Paris, or established themselves quickly through a migration of students from some other university, as in the cases of Padua, Vercelli, and Leipzig; but in either event the charters which gave them standing as *Studia Generalia*, and the privileges emanating from imperial, royal,

---

[1] Charter of Harvard College, 1650.
[2] Charter of Brown University, 1764.

princely, or papal authorities, were granted after, rather than before, masters and students had gathered for their work. The cases in which municipalities granted privileges to migrating bodies of students, before their coming, are not included in the above statement.

In some instances, however, civil and ecclesiastical authorities took the initiative. Among other examples of universities established directly by them may be cited Naples, founded by Emperor Frederick II, 1224; Toulouse, by Pope Gregory IX, 1230, 1233; Prague, by Emperor Charles IV, 1348; Caen, by Henry VI of England, 1432. The motives which led to this action were, on the one hand, the desire of political powers for the support of learned men, especially lawyers; and, on the other, the desire of the papacy for the more effective propagation of the Catholic faith.[1]

The political motive appears in the Letters-patent of Henry VI for Caen, 1432:

It befits Royal Highness to govern with due magnificence the peoples subject to him in times of wars and of peace, to the end that they may be defended valorously and constantly from the violence of enemies, and from wrongs offered them; and that they may be rendered tranquil and quiet through laws and active justice, by securing to each man his rights, with due regard to the common interests. For we think that this sort of justice, so excellent and advantageous, can never be practiced without the industry of men of great learning, steeped in laws, divine and human. And formerly our kingdom of France happily abounded in such men; but many kinds of evil men swarmed in, by whom, in the long process of time, the aforesaid kingdom, at one time through the disturbances of civil war, and

[1] See Compayre, "Abelard," pp. 41–45, and 35–41.

again through deadly pestilence, and finally through the various butcheries of men, and mighty famine — Alas ! the pity of it ! — has now been so shaken that scarcely can a sufficient number of sound justices be found in modern times, nor can others succeed, without great difficulty and personal peril, in acquiring securely knowledge and advancement, particularly in Civil Law ; whence the aforesaid kingdom, once governed with commendable justice, is subjected to greater inconveniences unless a wholesome remedy be shortly provided. . . .

We therefore, by our special favor, royal authority and plenary power, with the advice and consent of our distinguished Uncle John, governor and regent of our aforesaid kingdom of France and Duke of Bedford, and other nobles of our race, and of many wise men of our great council, do constitute, place, establish, found, and ordain forever by these present letters, a Studium Generale in our city of Caen, in the Diocese of Bayeux [Normandy].

The king does this for the better government of the kingdom, for the reason that no university exists within his jurisdiction in France, and for the preservation of the study of law :

We therefore, who with extreme longing desire to have our already-mentioned kingdom governed with justice and equity, and restored so far as we shall be able with God's help [to restore it] to its pristine glory, [establish this university] attentively considering the fact that no Studium in Civil Law has been established in our jurisdictions in France, and in the duchies of Normandy, Burgundy, and Brittany, the counties of Champagne and Flanders, the county of Picardy, and some other parts of the kingdom itself that are united in loyalty and obedience to us. [We do this] in order that the study of Civil Laws may not disappear in the aforesaid places, to the disadvantage of the State, but [that it] may become, under God's guidance, vigorous to His glory, and the glory of our aforesaid Kingdom, and may flourish as an ornament and an advantage to future times.

The city of Caen is selected for the location of the university because of its favorable position, character, and surroundings. It is

A city, forsooth, suitable, quiet, and safe, becomingly adorned with noted monasteries, fraternities, cloisters, and homes of the Mendicant Friars and other devout religious bodies; with an overflowing population of mild-dispositioned, obedient, and devout people; [a city] fit also because of its varied supply of food and other things adapted to the needs of the human race; prosperous and well-disposed, situated on fertile soil, and near the sea, so that students, and merchants as well, can more readily and easily come together there from almost all parts of the world.

The King grants to the university — in order to establish its prestige — all the privileges granted by royal authority to any other university in France:

And, that the Doctors, Licentiates, Bachelors, students, and dependents of the aforesaid university, and their households and domestic servants, may be able the more freely and quietly to devote themselves to letters and scholastic deeds, we will, by our royal authority and plenary power, bestow upon these same Doctors, Licentiates, Bachelors, students, dependents, households, and domestic servitors, such and similar privileges, franchises, and liberties as have been granted, given, and bestowed by our predecessors the kings of France upon the rest of the universities of our kingdom.

The king grants in particular the usual privilege of a special judge for cases affecting members of the university:

And as Conservator of these [privileges] henceforth, we depute and appoint our Bailiff of Caen now in office, and his successors or whoever may hold that office ; and to him we commit and consign by these present letters the hearing, determination, and final decision of cases and real actions [cases relating to conveyances of property] relating to persons and property, against all persons whatsoever who may be staying in our said Duchy of Normandy, or who may possess property there, either ecclesiastical or secular, if any action arises with regard to them, whether of offence or defence.

We command our justiciaries and officers, or those holding their places, one and all, to obey and to support efficiently the said Bailiff, the Conservator, or whoever holds his place, in the matters prescribed above, and such as are connected therewith. And that the foregoing regulations may acquire strength and firmness we have caused the present letters to be secured by the affixing of our seal.[1]

[1] Fournier, *Statuts*, etc., III, No. 1644.

IV

UNIVERSITY EXERCISES

THE ways and means of teaching in mediaeval universities were few and simple in comparison with those of our own times. The task of the student was merely to become acquainted with a few books and to acquire some facility in debate. The university exercises were shaped to secure this result. They consisted in the Lecture, the Disputation or Debate, the Repetition, the Conference, the Quiz, and the Examination.

Of these the first two and the last were by far the most important; they are described in detail below. The Repetition, given in the afternoon or evening, was either a detailed discussion of some point which could not be treated in full in the "ordinary" lecture, or a simple re-reading of the lecture, sometimes accompanied by catechism of the students upon its substance. The Conference was an informal discussion between professor and students at the close of a lecture, or a discussion of some portion of the day's work by students alone. The Quiz was often held in the afternoon at the student's hall or college, by the master in residence there, as described on page 132.

(a) *The Lecture*

Lectures were of two kinds, — "ordinary," and "extraordinary" or "cursory." The former were given in the morning, by professors; the latter in the afternoon, either by professors or by students about to take a bachelor's degree.

The purpose of the lecture was to read and explain the text of the book or books of the course. The character of the lecture was largely determined by the fact that all text-books, practically to the year 1500, were in manuscript, and by the further fact that many students seem to have been unable or unwilling to purchase or hire copies. A large part of the lecturer's time was thus consumed in the purely mechanical process of reading aloud the standard text and comments. To these he might add his own explanations; but the simple ability to " read the book " intelligently was sufficient to qualify a properly licensed Master, or a Bachelor preparing to take the Master's degree, to lecture on a given subject. This accounts for the fact that youths of seventeen or eighteen might be found giving occasional lectures, and that regular courses were given by those not much over twenty-one.

The books thus read consisted of two parts, — the text, and the " glosses " or comments. A glance at the selection on page 60 will reveal the nature of the latter: they were summaries, explanations, controversial notes, and cross-references, written by more or less learned scholars, in the margin of the text. In the course of generations the mass of glosses became so great as fairly to smother the original work. The selection just referred to is not especially prolific in glosses; cases may be found in which the text of a page occupies only three or four lines, the rest of the space being completely filled with comments, and with explanations of the comments. Instances of books explained to death are not unknown in our own class-rooms!

The effect of this accumulation of comments was to draw the attention of both teachers and students more and more away from the text. There is evidence that in some instances the text was almost wholly neglected in the attempt to master the glosses. University reforms at the end of the fifteenth and the beginning of the sixteenth century sometimes involved the exclusion of this mass of "frivolous and obscure" comment from the lectures, and a return to the study of the text itself. See the introduction to the plan of studies for Leipzig, p. 48.

The selection from the Canon Law (p. 59 ff.) gives a good idea of the substance of a dictated mediaeval lecture. Concerning the "original" and more or less offhand lecture we have the amusing account of Giraldus Cambrensis (*c.* 1146–1220), in his "most flattering of all autobiographies." After recounting — in the third person — his studies at Paris in Civil and Canon Law, and Theology, he says:

He obtained so much favor in decretal cases, which were wont to be handled Sundays, that, on the day on which it had become known throughout the city that he would talk, there resulted such a concourse of almost all the doctors with their scholars, to hear his pleasing voice, that scarcely could the amplest house have held the auditors.

And with reason, for he so supported with rhetorical persuasiveness his original, wide-awake treatment of the Laws and Canons, and so embellished his points both with figures and flowers of speech and with pithy ideas, and so applied the sayings of philosophers and authors, which he inserted in fitting places with marvellous cleverness, that the more learned and erudite the congregation, the more eagerly and attentively did they apply ears and minds to listening and memorizing. Of a truth they were led on and besmeared with words so sweet that, hanging, as it were, in suspense on the lips of the speaker, — though the address was long and involved, of a sort that is wont to be tedious to many, — they found it impossible to be fatigued, or even sated, with hearing the man.

And so the scholars strove to take down all his talks, word for word, as they emanated from his lips, and to adopt them with great eagerness. Moreover, on a certain day when the concourse from all parts to hear him was great, when the lecture was over and was followed by a murmur of favorable applause from all the throng, a certain distinguished Doctor who both had lectured on the Arts at Paris and long studied on the laws at Bologna, whose name was Master Roger the Norman, . . . broke out openly in expressions of this sort: "There is not such knowledge under the sun, and if it were by chance reported at Paris, it would, beyond a doubt, carry incomparable weight there, far more so than anywhere else." Now the opening — as it were, the proem — of that talk I have not considered it inappropriate to introduce here ; so this is the way it began :

"I had proposed to hear before being heard, to learn before speaking, to hesitate before debating. For to cultured ears and to men of the highest eloquence my speech will appear to have little marrow in its views, and its poverty of words will seem jejune. For idle is it, and utterly superfluous, to offer that which is arid to the eloquent, and that which is stale to men of knowledge and wisdom. Whence our Moral Seneca, and, quoting from him, Sidonius, says:

"'Until Nature has drunk in knowledge, it is not greater glory to speak what you know than to be silent about what you do not know.'

"And yet, since, on the testimony of Augustine, 'Every part out of harmony with its whole is base,' that I may not seem the sole anomaly among you, or, where others speak, be found by my silence a disciple of Pythagoras surpassing the rest, I have chosen to be found ridiculous for my speaking, rather than out of harmony for my silence.

"What note then shall the noisy goose emit in the presence of the clear-songed swans? Shall he offer new things, or things well known? Things often considered and trite generate disgust; new things lack authority. For, as Pliny says : 'It is an arduous task to give novelty to old things, authority to new things, brightness to things obsolete, charm to things disdained, light to obscure things, credence to doubtful things, and to all things naturalness !'

"The question which we have before us is old, but not inveterate, — a question often argued, but whose decision is still pending : Should a Judge decide according to the evidence, or according to his conviction?"

Now he supported the second, but far less justifiable view, by arguments taken from the Laws and the Canons, so forcible that, while all were amazed, all were uncertain whether greater praise should be given to the ornateness of the words or to the efficacy of the arguments.[1]

The mode of lecturing on Roman Law at Bologna is thus described by Odofredus (*c.* 1200–1265), a distinguished teacher:

First, I shall give you summaries of each title [i. e., each chapter into which the books are divided] before I proceed to the text ; second, I shall give you as clear and explicit a statement as I can of the purport of each Law (included in the title) ; thirdly, I shall read the text with a view to correcting it ; fourthly, I shall briefly repeat the contents of the Law ; fifthly, I shall solve apparent contradictions, adding any general principles of Law (to be extracted from the passage), commonly

[1] Giraldus Cambrensis, ed. Brewer, I, pp. 45–47.

called " Brocardica," and any distinctions or subtle and useful
problems (*quaestiones*) arising out of the Law, with their solutions, as far as the Divine Providence shall enable me.   And
if any Law shall seem deserving, by reason of its celebrity or
difficulty, of a Repetition, I shall reserve it for an evening
Repetition.[1]

The varied statement and restatement of the passage,
implied in the foregoing description, was doubtless necessary to make it intelligible to the not-too-keen minds of
the auditors.   As Rashdall points out, it " makes no
mention of a very important feature of all mediaeval
lectures, — the reading of the ' glosses.' "   This is mentioned in the Bologna statutes now to be cited.

There are numerous statutes on the mode of lecturing.
At Bologna, and doubtless elsewhere, professors seem to
have experienced the difficulty, not unknown to modern
teachers, of getting through the entire course within the
prescribed time.   The students, who regulated the conduct of their teachers, made stringent rules to prevent
this, and punished violations of them by fines large
enough to make professors take due caution :

We have decreed also that all Doctors actually lecturing
must read the glosses immediately after reading the chapter or
the law, unless the continuity of the chapters or of the laws requires otherwise, taking the burden in this matter on their own
consciences in accordance with the oath they have taken.   Nor,
with regard to those things that are not to be read, must they
yield to the clamor of the scholars. Furthermore we decree that
Doctors, lecturing ordinarily or extraordinarily, must come to
the sections assigned *de novo*, according to the regulations below.   And we decree, as to the close observance by them of the
passages, that any Doctor, in his ordinary lecturing in Canon

[1] Quoted by Rashdall, I, p. 219.

or Civil Law, must deposit, fifteen days before the Feast of Saint Michael, twenty-five Bologna pounds with one of the treasurers whom the rectors have appointed ; which treasurer shall promise to give said money to the rectors, or the general beadle in their name, all at once or in separate amounts, as he shall be required by them or by him.

The form, moreover, to be observed by the Doctors as to the sections is this : Let the division of the book into sections (*puncta*) be determined, and then let him be notified. [And if any Doctor fails to reach any section on the specified date he shall be fined three Bologna pounds, while for a second offense he shall be fined five pounds, and for a third and each succeeding violation of the rule, ten pounds.] And if the twenty-five pounds are exhausted, he must deposit in said place a second twenty-five pounds ; and the second deposit must be made within eight days from the time when the first was exhausted. . . .

We decree also that no Doctor shall hereafter exceed one section in one lecture. And if the contrary be done by any one he shall be charged with perjury and punished to the extent of three pounds, to be taken from the money deposited for the purpose ; and as often as the violation occurs, so often shall the penalty be inflicted, so long as the statute is in force ; and the Rector also must exact it.

We add that at the end of a section the Doctors must announce to the scholars at what section they are to begin afterwards, and they shall be obliged to follow that section which they have begun, even to the end of the section. But if by chance, after due weight is given to the glosses or text, it seems useful to transfer a part of the lecture to another section, he shall be obliged in his preceding lecture to announce that to the scholars, so that those who wish may make provision beforehand ; under penalty of five Bologna shillings for each occasion for the Doctor who does to the contrary.

We order this statute to be published in each school at the beginning of the term. . . .

8

Since topics not read by the Doctors are completely neglected and consequently are not known to the scholars, we have decreed that no Doctor shall omit from his sections any chapter, decretal, law, or paragraph.   If he does this he shall be obliged to read it within the following section.   We have also decreed that no decretal or decree or law or difficult paragraph shall be reserved to be read at the end of the lecture if, through such reservation, promptness of exit at the sound of the appointed bell is likely to be prevented.[1]

A lecture might be either dictated or delivered rapidly, " to the minds rather than to the pens," of the auditors. For pedagogic and possibly other reasons, the latter method seems to have been preferred by the authorities; but lecturers, and students who desire to get full notes, seem to have insisted upon dictation.   A statute of the Masters of Arts at Paris, 1355, is one of several unsuccessful attempts to enforce rapid delivery:

Two methods of reading the books of the Liberal Arts have been tried: By the first, the Masters of Philosophy from their chairs rapidly set forth their own words, so that the mind of the listener can take them in, but his hand is not able to write them down ; by the second, they pronounce them slowly so that the listeners are able to write them down in their presence with the pen.   By diligent examination and mutual comparison of these ways the first method is found to be the better, because the conceptual power of the ordinary mind warns us to imitate it in our lectures.   Therefore, we, one and all, Masters of Arts, both lecturing and not lecturing, being especially convoked for this purpose. . . . have made a statute to this effect: All lecturers, Masters as well as Scholars, of the same Faculty, whenever and wherever they happen to be reading any book in regular order

[1] Malagola, *Statuti delle Università e dei Collegi dello Studio Bolognese.* Selections from pp. 41–43.

or course in the same Faculty, or to be discussing a question according to this or any other method of exposition, shall follow the former method of reading to the best of their ability, to wit : presenting it as though no one were writing it in their presence. It is in accordance with this method that discourses and recommendations are made in the University, and it is followed by Lecturers in the rest of the Faculties.

Transgressors of this Statute, whether Masters or Scholars, we deprive thenceforth of their positions as lecturers, of honors, offices, and the rest of their means of support under our Faculty, for one year. But if any one repeats the offense, we double the penalty for the first repetition ; for the second, we quadruple it, and so on. And auditors who interfere with the execution of this our Statute by shouting or whistling or raising a din, or by throwing stones, either personally or through their attendants or accomplices, or in any other way, we deprive of and cut off from our company for one year, and for each repetition we increase the penalty to twice and four times the length as above.[1]

(b) *The Disputation.*

The disputation, or debate, one of the most important university exercises, "first became really established in the schools as a result of the new method." (Cf. page 35.) This exercise was sometimes carried on in the manner of a modern debate; to " respond " in the schools (i. e., to defend a thesis in public debate), and to " oppose " (i. e., to argue against the respondent), was a common requirement for all degrees. Scholars and masters frequently posted in public places theses to the argument of which they challenged all comers, just as a knight might challenge all comers at a tournament to combat. In such cases the respondent usually indicated the side of the

[1] Bulaeus, *Historia Universitatis Parisiensis*, IV, 332.

question which he would defend. This practice, in a modified form, still exists in some European universities in the public examinations for the Doctor's degree.

In another mode, the disputation was carried on by a single person, who argued both sides of the question and drew the conclusion in favor of one side or the other. This was of course merely the oral use of the method of exposition commonly found in the works of scholastic philosophers and theologians. The lecture of Giraldus Cambrensis described above (page 109) was doubtless of this type. A complete example is to be found in Dante's " Quaestio de Aqua et Terra." The brief of the arguments on both sides of this question is here reproduced with some modifications. It illustrates not only the exercise itself, but also the ponderous complications which the scholastic method received at the hands of Abelard's successors, and the weakness of that method when applied to questions of natural science. The reader will note that the argument no longer proceeds by the simple citation of authorities pro and con; the reasonings of the debater are also introduced. Moreover, the argument is more complex. It involves first the statement of the affirmative position; second, the refutation of the affirmative by observation and by reasoning; third, objections to the refutation by reasoning; fourth, refutation of these objections; fifth, final refutation of the original arguments.

Introduction : Author's reasons for undertaking the discussion.

Let it be known to you all that, whilst I was in Mantua, a certain Question arose, which, often argued according to appearance rather than to truth remained undetermined. Wherefore, since from boyhood I have ever been nurtured in love of truth, I could not bear to leave the Question I have spoken of undiscussed: rather I wished to demonstrate the truth concerning it, and likewise, hating untruth as well as loving truth, to refute contrary arguments. And lest the spleen of many, who, when the objects of their envy are absent, are wont to fabricate lies, should behind my back transform well-spoken words, I further wished in these pages, traced by my own fingers, to set down the conclusion I had reached and to sketch out, with my pen, the form of the whole controversy.

THE QUESTION: IS WATER, OR THE SURFACE OF THE SEA, ANYWHERE HIGHER THAN THE EARTH, OR HABITABLE DRY LAND?

AFFIRMATIVE ARGUMENT: Five affirmative arguments generally accepted.

Reason 1. Geometrical Proof: Earth and Water are spheres with different centers; the center of the Earth's sphere is the center of the universe; consequently the surface of the Water is above that of the Earth.

Reason 2. Ethical Proof: Water is a nobler element than Earth; hence it deserves a nobler, or higher, place in the scheme of the universe.

Reason 3. Experimental Proof: based on sailors seeing the land disappear under their horizon when at sea.

Reason 4. Economical Proof: The supply of Water, namely, the sea, must be higher than the Earth; otherwise, as Water flows downwards, it could not reach, as it does, the fountains, lakes, etc.

Reason 5. Astronomical Proof: Since Water follows the moon's course, its sphere must be excentric, like the moon's excentric orbit; and consequently in places be higher than the sphere of Earth.

NEGATIVE ARGUMENT: These reasons unfounded.

I. REFUTATION BY OBSERVATION.

Water flows down to the sea from the land; hence the sea cannot be higher than the land.

II. REFUTATION BY REASONING:

    A. *Water cannot be higher than the dry land.*

        Proof: Water could only be higher than the Earth,

            1. If it were excentric, or

            2. If it were concentric, but had some excrescence.

            But since

                x. Water naturally moves downwards, and

                y. Water is naturally a fluid body:

            1. Cannot be true, for three impossibilities would follow:

                a. Water would move upwards as well as downwards;

                b. Water and Earth would move downwards in different directions;

                c. Gravity would be taught ambiguously of the two bodies.

            Proof of these impossibilities by a diagram.

            2. Cannot be true, for

                a. The Water of the excrescence would be diffused, and consequently the excrescence could not exist:

                b. It is unnecessary, and what is unnecessary is contrary to the will of God and Nature.

    B. *All land is higher than the sea.*

        Proof: It has been shown that Water is of one level, and concentric with the Earth:

        Therefore, since the shores are higher than the

edges of the sea, and since the shores are the lowest portions of the land,

It follows that all the land is higher than the sea.

C. *Objections to the foregoing reasoning, and their refutation.*

    1. *Possible affirmative argument :* Earth is the heaviest body ; hence it is drawn down to its own center, and lies beneath the lighter body, Water.

    2. *Objection to this argument :* Earth is the heaviest body only by comparison with others ; for Earth is itself of different weights.

    3. *Refutation of this objection :* On the contrary, Earth is a simple body, and as such subject to be drawn equally in every part.

    4. *Answer to the refutation, with minor objections and their refutation.*

        Since the objection is in itself sound, and Earth by its own Particular Nature, due to the stubbornness of matter, would be lower than the sea ; and since Universal Nature requires that the Earth project somewhere, in order that its object, the mixture of the elements, may be fulfilled :

It follows that there must be some final and efficient cause, whereby this projection may be accomplished.

    a. The final cause has been seen to be the purpose of Universal Nature.

    b. The efficient cause cannot be (i) the Earth, (ii) the Water, (iii) the Air or Fire, (iv) the heaven of the Moon, (v) the Planets, nor (vi) the Primum Mobile :

    Therefore it must be ascribed to the heaven of the Fixed Stars (for this has variety in efficiency, as is seen in the various constellations), and in particular to those Stars of the Northern Hemisphere which overhang the dry land.

> > (x) *First objection:* Why is the projecting continent then, not circular, since the motion of these stars is circular?
> >
> > *Answer:* Because the material did not suffice for so great an elevation.
> >
> > (y) *Second objection:* Why is this elevation in this particular place?
> >
> > *Answer:* Because God whose ways are inscrutable, willed it so.
> >
> > We should therefore desist from examining too closely the reasons, which we can never hope to fathom.
>
> D. *Refutation of the original arguments:*
>
> > *Reason 1.* Invalid because Earth and Water are spheres with the same center.
> >
> > *Reason 2.* Invalid because of the external influence of Universal Nature, counteracting the internal influence of Particular Nature.
> >
> > *Reason 3.* Invalid because it is sphericity of the sea and not the lowness of the land which interferes with one's view at sea.
> >
> > *Reason 4.* Invalid because Water does not flow to the tops of mountains, but ascends thither in the form of vapors.
> >
> > *Reason 5.* Invalid because Water imitating the moon in one respect, need not imitate it in all.[1]

This brief obviously illustrates much more than the form of the mediaeval Disputation. It leaves one in no doubt as to the difference between the natural science of the Middle Ages and that of our own time. It also illustrates the weakness of the scholastic method when applied to questions which modern science would settle by experiment. The argument abounds in misstatements

[1] Dante, *Quaestio de Aqua et Terra*, tr. A. C. White, pp. VII–IX.

of fact, the conclusion is incorrect, and the " reasoning " by which it is reached can be described, from the modern point of view, only as grotesque. The weakness of the method was recognized by Roger Bacon so early as the thirteenth century. The growing recognition of its futility finds repeated expression in the sixteenth and seventeenth centuries, notably in the New Method (Novum Organum) of Francis Bacon.

Like the scholastic method and the worship of Aristotle, the Disputation fell into disrepute because of the extravagant lengths to which it was carried. The following sarcastic criticism by the Spanish scholar, Juan Luis Vives (1462–1540), is one illustration of the growing revolt of his times against it :

Disputations, also, to no slight degree have blinded judgment. They were instituted originally (but only among young men) to stimulate mental vigor, often torpid, and to make young men keener in their studies, so that they might either conquer or not be conquered, and also that the instruction received from their teachers might be more deeply impressed upon them.

Among men, or older persons, there was a kind of comparison of opinions and reasons, not aimed at victory but at unravelling the truth. The very name testifies that they are called disputations because by their means the truth is, as it were, pruned or purged [dis = apart; puto = to prune, or to cleanse]. But after praise and reward came from listeners to the one who seemed to have the best ideas, and out of the praise often came wealth and resources, a base greed of distinction or money took possession of the minds of the disputants, and, just as in a battle, victory only was the consideration, and not the elucidation of truth. So that they defended strenuously whatever they once had said, and overthrew and trampled upon their adversary.

Low and sordid minds such as with drooping heads look solely at such trivial and ephemeral results, regarded as of small consequence the great benefit that results from study : — namely probity or knowledge of truth ; and these two things they did not regard with sufficient acuteness nor did they comprehend their great value, but they sought the immediate reward of money or popular favor.

And so, in order to get a greater return for their labor, they admitted the populace to their contests like the spectators of a play brought out at the theatre. Then, as one might expect when the standard is lowered, the philosopher laid aside his dignified, venerable character, and put on his stage dress that he might dance more easily : the populace was made spectator, umpire, and judge, and the philosopher did that which the flute player does not do on the stage, — he suited his music, not to his own ideas and to the Muses, as his old teacher advises, but wholly to the circle of onlookers and the crowd whence distinction and gain was likely to come back to the actors.

There was no need of real, solid teaching (at least, not in the opinion of those who are going to learn) ; but pretence and dust were thrown in the eyes of the crowd. So the one plain road of obtaining the truth was abandoned ; six hundred ways of pretending were made, by which each strove for what suited himself, especially since there is nothing made so ugly as to lack a sponsor.

Not only did the populace flock to this opinion — that the object of learning is to dispute, just as it is the object of military life to fight — but the public unanimity swept away the veterans, the *triarii* [the more experienced soldiers who were placed in the third line] as it were, of the scholastic campaign (but these have no more ability and judgment than the dregs of the people), so that they regard him as superfluous and foolish who would call them back to mental activity and character and that quiet method of investigation, philosophy. [They think that] there is no other fruit of studies save to keep your wits about you and not give way to your adversary, either to attack him boldly or to bear up against him, and shrewdly to contrive by what vigor, by what skill, by what method of supplanting, he may be overturned. Therefore under this beautiful scheme, surpassing all others, it was the plan to break in the boy immediately and train him constantly ; they began disputing as soon as they were born and ceased only at death. The boy brought to school, is bidden to dispute forthwith on the first day and is already taught to quarrel, before he can yet speak at all. So also in Grammar, in the Poets, in the Historians, in Logic, in Rhetoric, in absolutely every branch. Would any one wonder what they can find to do in matters that are perfectly open, very simple and elementary? There is nothing so transparent, so limpid that they do not cloud it over with some petty question as if ruffled by a breeze. It is [thought] characteristic of the most helpless stupidity, not to find something which you may make obscure by most intricate measures and involve in very hard and rigid conditions, which you may twist and twist again. For you may simply say : " Write to me," — here comes a question, if not from Grammar then from Logic, if not from Logic then from Physics, — " What motions are made in writing?" Or, from Metaphysics, " Is it substance or quality?"

And these boys are hearing the first rudiments of Logic who were only yesterday, or the day before, admitted to the school. So they are to be trained never to be silent, but vigorously to assert whatever comes uppermost lest they may seem at any time to have given in. Nor is one dispute a day enough, nor two, like a meal. At lunch they dispute, after lunch they dispute, at dinner they dispute, after dinner they dispute. Do they do these things to learn, or to cook a new dish? They dispute at home, they dispute away from home. At a banquet, in the bath, in the tepidarium, at church, in the city, in the fields, in public, in private, in all places and at all times they dispute.

Courtesans in charge of a panderer do not wrangle so many times, or gladiators in charge of a trainer do not fight so many times for a prize as these do under their teacher of philosophy.

The populace, not self-restrained and serious, but fickle, barbarous, pugnacious, is wonderfully tickled with all this as with a mock battle.   So there are very many exceedingly ignorant men, utterly without knowledge of literature in any form, who take more pleasure in this form of show than in all else; and the more easily to win the fight, they employ a quick and prompt mode of fighting and deliver a blow every second, as it were, in order the more speedily to use up their foe.   They neither assail their adversary with uninterrupted argument nor can they endure prolonged talk from him.   If by way of explaining himself he should begin to enlarge, they raise the cry : " To the point ! To the point ! Answer categorically ! "   Showing how restless and flippant *their* minds are who cannot stand a few words. . . .

To such a degree did they go that instead of a settlement based on the strongest arguments, such as drove them into their absurdities, they considered it sufficient to say : " I admit it, for it follows from my own conclusion," and the next step is : " I deny it.   Prove it.   I will defend it appropriately."   For he who " defends appropriately "(in their own words), no matter by what incongruous admissions and concessions, is held to be a learned man and best adapted to disputation, that is, to the apex of all knowledge.

(c) *The Examination*

The examination, as an exercise leading to a degree, is one phase of modern educational practice which comes from mediaeval universities. The system of examinations grew up slowly. Generalization is difficult owing to the differences in practice in various universities, but broadly speaking the student who took a Master's or Doctor's degree in any Faculty passed through the three stages of Bachelor, Licentiate, and Doctor, and at each stage underwent some form of examination. The examination for the License (to teach anywhere) seems to have been the most formidable of the three ; that for the Doctorate being mainly ceremonial. In general, the examination tested the candidate's knowledge of the books prescribed, and his power of public debate.

The statutes of Bourges (c. 1468–1480) thus describe the requirements and the manner of procedure of examinations for the License in Arts :

[In preparation for the A. B. degree, which preceded the License, the candidate had heard lectures on (1) The Isagoge (Introduction) of Porphyry to the Categories of Aristotle, (2) the following works of Aristotle : (a) Categories ; (b) Peri Hermeneias (On Interpretation), the first (?) two books and a part of the fourth; (c) Topics, first book ; (d) Physics, first three books.]

Likewise we have decreed that before any one comes to the grade of License he must have heard four other books of Physics, three books " On the Heavens," two of " On Generation," the first three of " On Meteors," three " On the Soul," " On the Memory," " On the Length and Brevity of Life," with the first six books of " Metaphysics " and the first six on " Ethics " with a part of Euclid, and with the book " On the Sphere " [by John Sacrobosco].

Likewise we have decreed that candidates must respond twice openly and in public, and there may be five at most in one day and in the same debate ; yet four will be sufficient. And when they respond they must pay, each his own chairman, a scudo of gold.

Likewise we have determined that, when this has been done, the Faculty shall appoint four Masters who have already been Masters for three years and who do not have [the candidates] that year as pupils under their own special direction ; and they shall test the sufficiency of all the candidates. And the said committee shall take oath that they will accept those who are eligible and will reject those who are ineligible.

Likewise we have decreed that, when this has been done, on the report of said committee, over their seals manual faithfully transmitted, the Chancellor shall arrange the candidates in the order assigned to them by said committee, always putting the better men and those who are eligible ahead of the others, in order that the opportunity of studying well may be given to the students and that no one may suffer harm from his position.

Likewise we have decreed that before proceeding to license the candidates themselves, the assembled Faculty of Arts shall ordain four Masters, other than the first, who shall examine in assigned groups the said candidates in their own persons. And if they do not find them to be such as the first examiners reported that they found them, they shall report to the Faculty, pointing out the deficiency that the Faculty may have knowledge of the mistake of the first committee. If it finds that they made a mistake it shall have authority to correct their errors by changing the positions [of the names on the list] and by rejecting them entirely if they seem ineligible.

Likewise we have decreed that when their approval or disapproval has been settled by the said second examiners, they shall place their candidates according to proper order in one list sealed with their own seals, and shall deliver it, under enclosure, to the Chancellor, and it shall not be lawful for him to change the order but he shall license them in the order set down in the list.[1]

The process of taking the Licentiate and the Doctorate in Laws at Bologna, in vogue at the end of the thirteenth century and later, is described at great length in the Statutes of 1432. The examination consisted of two parts; the first private, the second public. The first led to a License, which was, however, a license merely to

[1] Document printed by Rashdall, II, Pt. II, pp. 742–3.

proceed to the public examination. The Statute concerning the private examination is summarized by Rashdall :

The private Examination was the real test of competence, the so-called public Examination being in practice a mere ceremony. Before admission to each of these tests the candidate was presented by the Consiliarius of his Nation to the Rector for permission to enter it, and swore that he had complied with all the statutable conditions, that he would give no more than the statutable fees or entertainments to the Rector himself, the Doctor or his fellow-students, and that he would obey the Rector. Within a period of eight days before the Examination the candidate was presented by "his own" Doctor or by some other Doctor or by two Doctors to the Archdeacon, the presenting Doctor being required to have satisfied himself by private examination of his presentee's fitness. Early on the morning of the examination, after attending a Mass of the Holy Ghost, the candidate appeared before the assembled College and was assigned by one of the Doctors present two passages (puncta) in the Civil or Canon Law as the case might be. He then retired to his house to study the passages, in doing which it would appear that he had the assistance of the presenting Doctor. Later in the day the Doctors were summoned to the Cathedral or some other public building by the Archdeacon, who presided over but took no active part in the ensuing examination. The candidate was then introduced to the Archdeacon and Doctors by the presenting Doctor or Promoter as he was styled. The Prior of the College then administered a number of oaths in which the candidate promised respect to that body and solemnly renounced all the rights of which the College had succeeded in robbing all Doctors not included in its ranks. The candidate then gave a lecture or exposition of the two prepared passages ; after which he was examined upon them by two of the Doctors appointed by the College. Other Doctors might ask supplementary questions of Law (which they

were required to swear that they had not previously communi-
cated to the candidate) arising more indirectly out of the passages selected, or might suggest objections to the answers.
With a tender regard for the feelings of their comrades at this
"rigorous and tremendous Examination" (as they style it) the
students by their Statutes required the Examiner to treat
the examinee "as his own son." The Examination concluded,
the votes of the Doctors present were taken by ballot and the
candidate's fate determined by the majority, the decision being
announced by the Archdeacon.[1]

The successful candidate ordinarily proceeded within
a short time to the public examination, which was held
in the cathedral. At this examination he received both
the formal license to teach and the Doctor's degree.
Before the appointed day he went about inviting friends
and public officials to the ceremony. Ostentation at
this time was forbidden:

Those who are candidates for the Doctor's degree, when
they give their invitations to the public examination, should go
without trumpets or any instruments whatever ; and the Beadle
of the Arch-deacon of Bologna, with the Beadles of the
Doctors under whom they are to have the public examination,
should precede him on horseback. At that late day they [the
candidates] shall not provide any feast, except among scholars
from the same house or among those related to the candidate
in the first, second, third, or even the fourth degree. Furthermore no one of the Rectors shall presume to ride with him on
that day.[2]

On the actual day of the examination, however, "the
love of pageantry characteristic of the mediaeval and

1 Rashdall, I, p. 226.
2 Malagola, *Statuti*, etc., p. 116.

especially of the Italian mind was allowed the amplest gratification"; the candidate went to the cathedral, doubtless preceded by trumpeters, and escorted by a procession of his fellow-students. The statutes of the German Nation at Bologna describe as one object of that organization "the clustering about, attendance upon, and crowding around our Doctors-to-be, in season and out of season." Moreover, "the Scholars of our Nation shall individually accompany the one who is to be made Doctor, to the place where the insignia [of the degree] are usually bestowed, if he so wishes, or has so requested of the Proctor [of the Nation]. Also, they shall escort him with a large accompanying crowd from the aforesaid place to his own house, under penalty of one Bologna shilling." [1]

The University statutes are to the same effect, but they prohibit horse-play, and the extravagance of tournaments. "Ultramontane" scholars are those from north, "Cismontane," those from south, of the Alps.

Moreover, the ultramontane scholars shall accompany the ultramontane candidate, and the cismontane, the cismontane, from their dwelling places to Saint Peter's when they go there to take the public examination, and at that time hay and straw shall not be placed [on the floor of] the church. Furthermore all the ultra- and cis-montanes shall be present at the public examination, and all shall afterwards accompany the new Doctor from the church to his house under penalty of ten Bologna shillings, which it shall be the duty of the Rector to exact within eight days. And no scholar at the public examination of any citizen or foreign scholar shall be dressed for a dance or a brawl or a tournament, nor shall he joust as a

[1] *Acta Nationis Germanicae*, pp. 4, 8.

knight.   If any one disobey, he shall incur the penalty of perjury and ten Bologna pounds, and if he does not pay this within
ten days on the demand of any Rector he shall be deprived of
the advantage and honor of our University.   And we impose the
penalty of perjury also upon the Rector of the student who is
to take the public examination, and this penalty he shall incur
from the very fact that he should by all means exact from the
candidate an oath that on the day on which he rides about to
give invitations for the public examination which he is to take,
he will not bring about any jousting or brawling as some have
done heretofore.   And if the candidate, when required, is unwilling to take the oath, or if he takes the oath and breaks it,
he [the Rector] shall utterly forbid the public examination and
direct the Doctors not to hold their meeting and also stop the
Beadle, so that he shall not dare to announce his programme
through the schools, under an arbitrary penalty to be imposed.[1]

The ceremony at the cathedral included, first, the
formal test of the candidate.   After making a speech he
held a disputation, in which he defended a thesis taken
from the Laws against opponents chosen from the body
of students, " thus playing for the first time the part of
a Doctor in a University disputation."   He was then
presented by the Promotor to the Archdeacon, who
conferred the final License to teach Civil or Canon Law
or both, according to the student's training.   This was
done by a formula probably similar to the following,
which is taken from a book published in 1710:

Inasmuch as you have been presented to me for examination
in both [Civil and Canon] Laws and for the customary approval, by the Most Illustrious and Most Excellent D. D.
(naming the Promoters), golden Knights, Counts Palatine,

[1] Malagola, *Statuti*, etc., p. 116.

Most Celebrated Doctors, and inasmuch as you have since undergone an arduous and rigorous examination, in which you bore yourself with so much learning and distinction that that body of Most Illustrious and Excellent Promoters without one dissenting voice, — I repeat, without one dissenting voice, — have judged you worthy of the laurel, therefore by the authority which I have as Archdeacon and senior Chancellor, I create, publish, and name you, N. N., Doctor in the aforesaid Faculties, giving to you every privilege of lecturing, of ascending the Master's chair, of writing glosses, of interpreting, of acting as Advocate, and of exercising also the functions of a Doctor here and everywhere throughout the world ; furthermore, of enjoying all those privileges which those happy individuals, who have been so deserving in these fostering colleges, are accustomed to use and enjoy.

And I trust that all these things will forever result in the increase of your fame and the honor of our Colleges, to the praise and glory of Almighty God and of the ever blessed Virgin Mary.[1]

" In pursuance of the license thus conferred, he was then invested by the Promotor with the *insignia* of the teaching office, [the chair, the book, the ring, the cap,] each, no doubt, with some appropriate formula. He was seated in the Magisterial chair or *cathedra*. He was handed the open book — one of the Law texts which it was his function to expound. A gold ring was placed upon his finger, either in token of his espousal to Science or in indication of the Doctor's claim to be the equal of Knights; and the Magisterial *biretta* placed upon his head: after which the Promotor left him with a paternal embrace, a kiss, and a benediction."[2] Then

[1] Document printed by Rashdall, II, Pt. II, p. 734.
[2] Rashdall, I, p. 229.

followed the triumphal procession homeward through the town, " preceded by the three University pipers and the four University trumpeters."

(d) *A Day's Work at Louvain in* 1476

Documents which describe the day's work of a mediaeval student are not common. A Ducal ordinance for the University of Louvain in 1476 indicates the way in which the student was supposed to work at that institution.

The tutors shall see that the scholars rise in the morning at five o'clock, and that then before lectures each one reads by himself the laws which are to be read at the regular lecture, together with the glosses. . . . But after the regular lecture, having if they wish, quickly heard mass, the scholars shall come to their rooms and revise the lectures that have been given, by rehearsing and impressing on their memory whatever they have brought away from the lectures either orally or in writing. And next they shall come to lunch . . . after lunch, each one having brought to the table his books, all the scholars of the Faculty together, in the presence of a tutor, shall review that regular lecture ; and in this review the tutor shall follow a method which will enable him, by discreet questioning of every man, to gather whether each of them listened well to the lecture and remembered it, and which will recall the whole lecture by having its parts recited by individuals. And if watchful care is used in this one hour will suffice.[1]

(e) *Time-table of Lectures at Leipzig,* 1519

There must have been some orderly arrangement of each day's lectures as the requirements for the various

[1] Document printed by Rashdall, Vol. II, Pt. II, p. 766.

degrees became fixed; but I have not found an early document on the subject. The Statutes of Leipzig for 1519 give "an accurate arrangement of the lectures of the Faculty of Fine Arts, hour by hour, adapted to a variety of intellects and to diverse interests." They do not always specify the semester in which the book is to be read; in such cases the title is placed in the center of the column. The list includes practically all the books required for the degrees of A. B. and A. M. Unless otherwise specified, they are the works of Aristotle; but the versions are, as noted on page 48, new translations from the Greek. These translations are praised in no uncertain terms in the Statutes. The Metaphysic is presented in Latin by Bessarion "so cleverly and with so good faith that he will seem to differ not even a nail's breadth from the Greek copies and sentiments of Aristotle." The Ethics and the Economics are "cleverly and charmingly put into Latin by Argyropulos;" the Politics and the Magna Moralia are "finely translated by Georgius Valla, that well-known man of great learning," etc. Lectures, it will be noted, began early. The following tabular view is compiled from Zarncke, *Statutenbücher der Universität Leipzig*, pp. 39–42.

In addition to the "ordinary," or prescribed, books, "two books of Cicero's Letters will be read on festal days"; and "the Greek Grammar of Theodorus Gaza will be explained at the expense of the illustrious Prince George."

SUMMER	WINTER	SUMMER	WINTER

6 A. M.

		1 P. M.

Metaphysics. | Metaphysics.
Introduction | On Interpreta-
(Porphyry). | tion.
Categories. | Logic (Aquinas).

On Six Principles (Gilbert de la
Porrée).
Physics (Digest of Aristotle by
Albertus Magnus).

Posterior Ana- | Topics (4 Bks.)
lytics. | Generation and
Sense and Sen- | Destruction.
sation. | Being and Es-
Memory and | sence (Aqui-
Recollection. | nas).
Sleep and Wak-
ing.
Longevity and
Shortlived-
ness.

8 A. M.

Physical Hearing (sic). Physics?
Reading and Disputation by can-
didates for A.B. and A.M.
Grammar (Priscian).

Institutes of Oratory (Quintilian).

2 P. M.

11 A. M.

On the Soul (3 | On the Heavens
Bks). | and the Earth.
Common Arith- | On the Sub-
metic, and On | stance of the
the Sphere | World (Aver-
(Sacrobosco). | roes).
| Common Per-
| spective, i.e.,
Logic: Summulae (Petrus Hispanus).

Rhetoric, (Cic- | On the Orator
ero to Heren- | (Cicero).
nius). | On the Vital
Physical Aus- | Principle (The-
cultation | mistius).
(Themistius). |

Optics (John
of Pisa).
Theory of the Planets (Gerard of
Cremona).
Ethics.
Politics.
Economics.
Magna Moralia, *i. e.*, Ethics, ab-
breviated from Aristotle and
Eudemus.

4 P. M.

Theocritus.
Herodotus.
Virgil.
Aristotle, Problems.

V

REQUIREMENTS FOR THE DEGREES IN ARTS

IN general, the candidate for the A. B. degree must
have taken part as "respondent" or "opponent" (see
p. 115) in a prescribed number of disputations, and must
have " heard " the lectures on certain prescribed books
before taking his examination for the degree. (This
examination seems, in some cases, to have been little
more than a certification by a committee of Masters
that the student had fulfilled the foregoing requirements.) The candidate for the degree of A. M. must
have completed further prescribed books and disputations, and must have " read," i. e., lectured upon, some
book or books which he had previously " heard," before
taking his examination for the License (to teach everywhere). No general statement can be given as to the
required number of disputations ; the practice differed
at various times and places. The Statutes of Leipzig
required during the fifteenth century six " ordinary " and
six " extraordinary " responses from the prospective
Bachelor. The prospective Master was required to
declare that he had been present at thirty ordinary
Bachelors' disputations, and had argued in each one " if
he had been able to get the opportunity to argue." The
candidate for the License at Paris, in 1366, must have
attended disputations throughout one " grand Ordinary,"
and must have " responded " twice. At Oxford the youth

must have taken part in disputations for a year as " general sophister," and must have " responded" at least once, before taking the A. B. or before " Determination," which was the equivalent of the A. B.   Prospective masters must have responded at least twice.[1]

The following lists of prescribed books give a good idea of mediaeval requirements (aside from disputations) for the degrees of A. B. and A. M., at various times and places.   The reader will note at once the predominance of Aristotle, and the variations in requirements for the degrees.   Many similar lists might be cited from the records of other universities; but they would give little additional information as regards the degrees in Arts.

1. List of Books Prescribed for the Degrees of A. B. and A. M. at Paris, 1254.

The following list from the Statutes of 1254 does not separate the books into the groups required for each degree, but indicates the total requirement for both.

(1) The "Old" Logic
- Introduction to the Categories of Aristotle (Isagoge), Porphyry.
- Categories, and On Interpretation, Aristotle.
- Divisions, and Topics except Bk. IV, Boethius.

(2) The "New" Logic
- Prior and Posterior Analytics, Aristotle.
- Sophistical Refutations,   "
- Topics,   "

(3) Moral Philosophy: Ethics, 4 Bks.,   "

[1] Statutes of 1431.

(4) Natural Philosophy	Physics,	Aristotle.
	On the Heavens and the Earth,	"
	Meteorics,	"
	On Animals,	"
	" the Soul,	"
	" Generation,	"
	" Sense and Sensible Things,	"
	" Sleep and Waking,	"
	" Memory and Recollection,	"
	" Life and Death,	"
	" Plants,	" (?)
(5) Metaphysics :	Metaphysics,	"
(6) Other Books	On the Six Principles, Gilbert de la Porrée.	
	Barbarismus (Bk. 3, Larger Grammar), Donatus.	
	Grammar (Major and Minor), Priscian.	
	On Causes, Costa ben Luca.	
	On the Differences of Spirit and Soul (another translation of On Causes).[1]	

An interesting part of the Statute of 1254 relates to the length of time to be given to the various books, or groups of books, prescribed. The entire Old Logic is to be read in about six months (October 1–March 25); the New Logic and Priscian's Grammar in the same length of time; the Physics, the Metaphysics and On Animals, together, in somewhat more than eight months (October 1–June 25); the four books of the Ethics, alone, in six weeks; On Life and Death is to be completed in one week, and several of the other treatises in the same group are to be read in periods varying from two to five weeks. Knowledge of these facts renders the list as a

[1] *Chart. Univ. Paris.*, I, No. 246.

whole considerably less imposing than it might otherwise appear.

2. Books required at Paris in 1366. In this and all the following examples the books are by Aristotle unless otherwise specified.

For the A. B. :

(1) Grammar: Doctrinale, Alexander da Villa Dei.
(2) Logic : The Old and the New Logic, as above.
(3) Natural Philosophy : On the Soul.

For the License to teach everywhere :

(1) Natural Philosophy : Physics ; On the Heavens and the Earth; On Generation and Corruption ; Parva Naturalia (see p. 143) ; On Mechanics.
(2) Mathematics : " Some books " ; probably the treatises required at Leipzig in 1410. (See p. 140).
(3) Politics.
(4) Rhetoric.

For the A. M. :

(1) Ethics.
(2) Meteorics (3 Bks.).[1]

3. Books required at Oxford, 1267: For the A. B. (Determination) :

(1) Logic : The Old and the New Logic (see p. 140), and On the Six Principles.
(2) Either Grammar (selections from Donatus and Priscian), or Natural Philosophy (Physics, On the Soul, and On Generation and Corruption).[2]

For the A. B. in (?) 1408.

(1) Logic : The Old and the New Logic in " cursory," or extraordinary, lectures, given by Bachelors ; Introduction, Por-

---

[1] Rashdall, I, p. 436.
[2] *Munimenta Acad. Oxon.*, I, pp. 35–36.

phyry : On the Six Principles, Gilbert de la Porrée ; Sophistical Refutations.

(2) Grammar ; Barbarismus, Donatus.

(3) Mathematics : Arithmetic ; Computus ecclesiasticus (Method of finding Easter) ; On the Sphere, Sacrobosco.[1]

4. Books required at Leipzig for the Degree of A. B. in 1410.[2]

(1) Grammar ; Priscian (the last two books). [2 months.]

(2) Logic { Tractatus (Summulae), Petrus Hispanus. [2½–3 months.]
The " Old " Logic (see Paris, 1254). [3–4 months.]
The " New " " except Topics. [6½–7 months.]

(3) Nat'l Philosophy { Physics. [6–9 months.]
On the Soul. [7 weeks–2 months.]

(4) Mathematics ; On the Material Sphere (Sacrobosco). [5–6 weeks.]

5. Books required at Leipzig for the Degree of A. M. in 1410.

(1) Logic { Logic of Heytisbury.
Topics, Aristotle. [3–4 months.]

(2) Moral and
Practical
Philosophy { Ethics. [6–9 "]
Politics. [4–9 "]
Economics. [3 weeks.]

(3) Natural Philosophy { On the Heavens and the Earth. [3½–4 months.]
On Generation and Destruction. [7 weeks–2 months.]
Meteorics. [3½–4 months.]
Parva Naturalia (i. e., the books on Sense and Sensible Things, Sleep and Waking, Memory and Recollection, Longevity and Shortlivedness). [2½–3 months.]

[1] *Munimenta Acad. Oxon.*, I, pp. 242–243.

[2] The figures in brackets indicate the time to be given to each book, or group of books. The data are from Zarncke, *Statutenbücher der Univ. Leipzig.*, pp. 311–312.

(4) Metaphysics :   Metaphysics. [5–9 months.]

(5) Mathematics   { Astronomy : Theory of the Planets (Gerard of Cremona). [5–6 weeks.]
Geometry : Euclid. [5–9 months.]
Arithmetic : Common Arithmetic (Sacrobosco). [3 weeks–1 month.]
Music : Music (John de Muris). [3 weeks–1 month.]
Optics : Common Perspective (John of Pisa). [3–3½ months.] [1]

[1] For the requirements in 1519 see p. 134.

VI

ACADEMIC LETTERS

1. LETTERS RELATING TO PARIS

(a) *A Twelfth-Century Critic*

THE pessimist who laments the decay of education, and who feels that its golden age was the time in which he received his own training, or earlier, is a perennial figure in the history of education. The following letter has a surprisingly modern ring. Denifle (p. 747) thinks that Stephen was unable to reconcile himself to the new movement at Paris because of his monastic training. Stephen's view, however, " was not wholly wrong." Compare the letter of Peter de la Celle to John of Salisbury, page 144.

" Stephen [Bishop] of Tournai, in his letters directed to the Pope, laments the ruin of the study of sacred literature, of Canon Law and the Arts, and, blaming the professors, implores the hand of Apostolic correction." (1192–1203.)

To the Pope. Beseeching his pardon, we would speak to our sovereign Pontiff, whose kindness stimulates our boldness, whose knowledge supports our ignorance, whose patience assures indulgence. The authority of our forefathers first impels us, then the disease which is insinuating itself, and which will in the end be irremediable if its evil influence be not checked at the beginning. Nor do we say this, Father, as though we wish

to be either censors of morals, or judges of the doctors, or de-
baters of doctrines.   This burden requires stronger shoulders
and this fight calls for the vigorous arms of spiritual athletes.
We wish only to point out this distress to your sacred Father-
hood, on whom God has conferred the power of checking error
and the knowledge of how to correct it.

The study of sacred letters among us has descended into the
very factory of confusion ; the teachers are more watchful for
glory than for doctrine, and they write up new and modern
summaries and commentaries upon theological foundations,
with which they soothe, retain, and deceive their pupils ; as
though there were not plenty of works of the holy fathers
who, we read, put forth their sacred writings inspired by that
same spirit which we believe inspired the apostles and prophets
when they composed theirs. . . . Public debates are carried
on in violation of the sacred constitutions concerning the in-
comprehensibility of the Deity ; a wordy, carnal strife on the
incarnation of the Word goes on irreverently.   Even the indi-
visible Trinity is divided at the street corners and quarrelled
over, so that there are already as many errors as there are teachers, as many scandals as lecture rooms, as many blasphemies as
public squares.

Furthermore, if recourse is had to the courts which are
established by Common Law, either those set up by us, or
by the regular judges which we are bound to recognize, there
is presented by venal men the tangled forest of the Decretals,
under the pretext, as it were, of the sacred memory of Pope
Alexander, and the more ancient sacred Canons are thrown
away, rejected, and spewed out.

This confusion being made in the very centre of the wholesome regulations made by the Councils of the holy fathers, they
impose upon their councils no method and on their business no
restraint, those letters having prevailing weight, which, it may
be, lawyers have forged and engrossed for pay in their own
offices or chambers.   A new volume, got together from these
sources, is both read regularly in the schools and is exposed for

sale in the market with the approval of the crowd of notaries, who rejoice that both their labor is lessened and their pay increased in engrossing these suspicious works.

Two woes have been set forth, and lo, a third woe remains! The Faculties called liberal [i. e., free] have lost their old time liberty, and are devoted to a slavery so complete that long-haired youths shamelessly possess themselves of the offices in these Faculties, and beardless boys sit in the seat of the Elders, and those who do not yet know how to be pupils strive to be named Doctors. And they themselves compile their own summaries, reeking and wet with [their own] further drivellings, and not even seasoned with the salt of the philosophers. Neglecting the rules of the Arts and throwing away the standard works of the Makers of the Arts, they catch in their sophisms, as in spiders' webs, the midges of their empty trifling phrases. Philosophy cries out that her garments are rent and torn asunder; she modestly covers her nakedness with certain carefully prepared remnants [but] she is neither consulted by the good man nor does she console the good woman.

These things, O Father, demand the hand of Apostolic correction, that the present unseemliness of teaching, learning, and debating may by your authority be reduced to definite form, that the Divine Word may not be cheapened by vulgar attrition; that it may not be said on the corners, Lo! Here is Christ, or Lo! He is there! that sacred things may not be cast before dogs or pearls before swine to be trampled under their feet.[1]

(b) *The Monastic View*

To many of the monks of this period study and the search for truth through reason were repellent. In their view the way to spiritual truth was through retirement from the world, and the observance of religious exercises. This is the burden of a letter to John of Salisbury by Peter de la Celle, abbot of a monastery

[1] *Chart. Univ. Paris.*, I, f. 47.

near Rheims, in 1164. Incidentally it gives his view concerning Paris.

" Peter de la Celle to John of Salisbury concerning the perils that encompass souls at Paris and concerning the true school of truth."

His own Abbot to his own clerk. You have, my well-beloved, chosen a sufficiently delightful exile, where joys, though they be vain, are in superabundance, where the supply of bread and wine exceeds in richness that of your own land where there is the frequent access of friends, where the dwelling together of comrades is common. Who else besides you is there beneath the sky who has not thought Paris the place of delights, the garden of plantations, the field of first fruits?

Yet, though smiling [at these things], you have said truly that where pleasure of the body is greater and fuller, there is the exile of the soul; and where luxury reigns there the soul is a wretched and afflicted hand-maid. O Paris! How well-suited art thou to captivate and deceive souls! In thee are the nets of the vices, in thee the arrow of Hell transfixes the hearts of the foolish! This my John has felt and therefore he has named it an exile. Would that you were leaving behind that exile of yours just as it is, and were hastening to your native land not in word and tongue only but in very deed and truth! There, in the book of life would you be looking, not upon forms and elements, but upon divinity itself, as it really is, as upon truth — eye to eye, without labor of reading, without tediousness of seeing, without fallacies and mistakes of understanding, without anxiety of retaining, without fear of forgetting. O blessed school, where Christ teaches our hearts with the words of his virtue, where without study and lecture we learn how we should live happily to eternity! There no book is bought, no teacher of things written is hired, there is no circumventing in debate, no intricacy of sophisms, [but] a plain settlement of all questions, a full apprehension of universal reasons and arguments. There life avails more than lecture; simplicity, more than cavilling. There no one is shut in [i. e., limited in freedom] save he who is shut out. In a word; there every reproach is done away with in the answer given to him who evilly presents an evil life: "Depart from me, ye cursed, into everlasting fire prepared for the devil and his angels;" and to him who sets for a good life: "Come, ye blessed" &c.

Would that the sons of men were as intent upon these better studies as they are on idle talking, on vain and base buffoonery! Certainly they would harvest richer fruits, more excellent favors, certainly greater honors and beyond doubt would learn the end of all perfection, — Christ, — whom they will never find in these. Farewell.[1]

(c) *Letters from or to Students at Paris*

These letters belong to a period covering nearly four centuries. The first gives an opinion of William of Champeaux in marked contrast to that of Abelard.

(1) A Certain D. writes to a Certain Prior concerning his Studies at Paris. (1109–1112.)

I am now in Paris in the School of Master William of Champeaux, the greatest of all the men of his time whom I have known, in every branch of learning. When we hear his voice we think that no man, but, as it were, an angel from heaven, is speaking; for the melody of his words and the profundity of his ideas transcends, as it were, human limitations. . . .

Here, my revered friend, I am training my youth that I may not utterly succumb to those vices which, unless conquered, are wont, as a rule, to overturn this period of life. Here I am doing my best to illumine by doctrine and study my untaught mind, emancipated from the shades of ignorance and the sin of the first man, so far as God, from whom alone comes every

---

[1] *Chart. Univ. Paris.*, I, No. 22, p. 24.

blessing of wisdom, shall himself deign to permit.   Because the blessing of wisdom, when sought and acquired with pure interest, is rightly believed and considered by all men of discernment as the summum [bonum].   For, as the Apostle says: Knowledge without charity puffeth up but, with charity edifieth : for it uproots vices and grafts in virtues ; it instructs itself in its duty to itself, its neighbor, and its Creator ; finally, by its presence, it fortifies and defends the mind, over which it presides in person, against all the ills of this life that come to it from without.[1]

(2) Philip of Harvengt to Hergald, a Student at Paris (Date between 1154 and 1181)

Know that I have both read carefully and when read, accepted gratefully the letters which your affection, with memorable feeling, led you to send to me. . . . because in them I thought I saw evidence of your progress in learning. . . . Just as the Queen of Sheba is said to have come with a large retinue, that by the sight of her own eyes she might have surer knowledge of those things whose fame she had eagerly absorbed from afar, so you too, drawn by love of knowledge, came to Paris and found a much desired model of Jerusalem, sought for by many.   For here David strikes his harp of ten chords, here with mystic touch he composes the psalms.   Here Isaiah is read and in the reading his prophecies are revealed ; here the rest of the prophets present their diverse strains of harmonious melody.   Here the wisdom of Solomon is open for the instruction of those who have gathered from all parts of the world ; here his treasure house is thrown open to eager students.   Here to stimulate so great a concourse of students there is so great a throng of clerks that it vies with the numerous multitude of the laity.   Happy city! in which the Sacred Codes are pored over with so much zeal and their involved mysteries are solved by the gift of the outpoured Spirit, in which there is so

[1] Jaffé, *Bibliotheca*, V, pp. 285, ff.

much diligence on the part of the readers, and, in short, so much knowledge of Scriptures that it truly deserves to be called Cariath Sepher, that is The City of Letters. Therein would I have you instructed like Gothoniel, not so much in letters as in the spirit, and so to grasp the Scriptures that you may take delight in searching out their inner sweetness. . . . Farewell.[1]

(3) DESCRIPTION OF PARIS ABOUT 1175 BY GUY DE BASOCHES

To a youth who is noble and so like himself as to be a second self, Guy de Basoches [seeks] to match his nobility of birth by high-bred manners. . . .

My situation then is this : I am indeed in Paris, happy because of soundness of both mind and body, happier were you enjoying it too, and happiest had it but been my lot to have you with me. I am indeed in Paris, in that City of Kings, which not only holds, by the sweet delight of her natural dowry, those who are with her, but also alluringly invites those who are far away. For as the moon by the majesty of its more brilliant mirror overwhelms the rays of the stars, not otherwise does said city raise its imperial head with its diadem of royal dignity above the rest of the cities. It is situated in the lap of a delightful valley, surrounded by a coronet of mountains which Ceres and Bacchus adorn with fervent zeal. The Seine, no humble stream amid the army of rivers, superb in its channel, throwing its two arms about the head, the heart, the very marrow of the city, forms an island. Two suburbs reach out to right and left, the less excellent, even, of which begets envy in envious cities. From the two suburbs two stone bridges stretch over to the island and one of them which has been named for its size, for it is Great, faces the north and the English Sea, while the opposite one, which opens towards the Loire, they call the Little Bridge. . . .

On this island Philosophy, of old, placed a royal throne for herself, Philosophy, who, despised in her solitude, with a sole at-

<hr>

[1] *Chart. Univ. Paris.*, I, No. 51, p. 50.

tendant, Study, now possesses an enduring citadel of light and immortality, and under her victorious feet tramples the withered flowers of a world already in its dotage.

On this island, the seven sisters, to wit, the Liberal Arts, have secured an eternal abiding place for themselves, and, with the ringing clarion of their nobler eloquence, decrees and laws are proclaimed.

Here the healing fount of learning gushes forth, and as it were evoking from itself three most limpid streams, it makes a threefold division of the knowledge of the sacred page into History, Allegory and Morals.[1]

(4) Johann von Jenzenstein to Master Benesch of Horschowitz, concerning Paris. (1375.)

Master Bennessius, dearest comrade and friend. If recent doings at Paris are unknown to you, if the fecundity of pleasures, the abundance of all things edible, the manners of the men, the bountiful supply of all the sciences, even the clever teaching in very many material crafts, — if you could but see the mere shadow of all these, surely, overpowered by their arguments, you would throw off your sluggishness and generously enter into the aforesaid enjoyments ; and your eyes, grown old in old sights would renew their youth in these new sights. . . .

For here [says the writer sarcastically] are distinguished doctors of many faculties, some of whom by their crazy ways of thinking, and still others by crazy ways of acting, others, indeed, by inflicting wounds, and still others by abusive words, furnish enjoyment that is exceeding pleasing; and [he adds more seriously] there are other Masters subtly trained in the seven liberal Arts, by whose example and teaching the entire earth, like the heavens, is adorned with stars ; and some of these masters are illuminated by the three trivials and some by the four quadrivials and some by both the trivials and the quadrivials.

[1] *Bulletin de la Société de l'Histoire de Paris*, 1877, p. 37 f.

Now the three trivials are grammar, which teaches clearly the agreement of speech; and starting from that, the youth who holds on to his first teaching makes a beginning whereby he may obtain a deeper taste of the profundities of other knowledge also; the second is rhetoric, which by the charm of its colors adorns as with pearls the subject matter, and ennobles grammar, and instils acceptably into the ears of men that which is heard; the third is logic by means of which the method of skilful deductive reasoning is assigned to the individual sciences, without which the powers of all the sciences are quiescent, and by whose addition all the sciences are regularly organized. [The letter ends with a similar description of the quadrivials.] [1]

2. TWO OXFORD LETTERS OF THE FIFTEENTH CENTURY

(1) OXFORD UNIVERSITY TO THE DUKE OF GLOUCESTER, ACKNOWLEDGING A GIFT OF BOOKS. [1439.]

Most illustrious, most cultured and magnificent Prince, the enduring value of the benefits you have conferred on the English nation, and the meritorious deeds of your most powerful Highness in its behalf can never die, but, with distinguished fame destined to endure, will flourish with ever-renewed praise and happy remembrance. How delightful it certainly is for us to reflect upon these again and again! Among the rest, however, that deed itself redounds to the splendor of your most mighty Highness, namely, that after having brought about the repression of heretic plotting against the church of God, you have chosen to reinvigorate the vineyard of the Lord, your handmaid, the University of Oxford, with books on all the sciences and virtues, out of which the abundant wine of knowledge and truth may be squeezed by the press of study. For this reason we set forth in this humble letter our thanks, our praise, and our prayers, but we cannot express ourselves adequately.

[1] *Archiv für oesterreichische Geschichte*, Vol. 55, p. 385.

Which of the Universities has found a Prince so munificent, so illustrious, so magnificent? — whose service in the field has ever been successful, whose mind is most liberal, and who displays charity to all, justice to each, and harm to none. What respecter of the wise was ever so pious, what supporter of them so efficient, what patron of the sciences, of virtues, and of books so generous? And by these not only are the hearts of the living enlightened to the glory of God and the advance of virtue, but even more in coming ages will posterity be illumined. Can the happy memory of deeds so great pass away? Nay, but it will be a benediction forever.

A statute has been made in the words of your supplicant, and is to be forever in force, which will never fail in prayers in your behalf but will serve as an enduring memorial. Wherefore, although the fame of others may ebb with the flow of time or perish through being overshadowed by the rising of greater men, yet your fame cannot perish under the cloud of oblivion nor can it, of a truth, be obscured by the shadow of greater benefactions.

If the great conquests of Alexander come to our ears, renewed day by day through the devices of the wise Greeks who committed such deeds to writing, how much more will this University, your devoted supplicant, bear witness to your magnificent deeds to the end of time, not only by her prayers but also in her writings? Nay, were the tongues of all to be silent the fact itself would bear witness more than speech, the fact, to wit, that one hundred and thirty-nine most precious volumes of theology, medicine, and the seven liberal sciences have been deposited in our library from your own collection, as an eternal witness to your surpassing virtues and munificence.

We pray therefore that you may be willing to look upon this University as your vineyard and your handmaid and perpetual supplicant. And may the Lord Himself most glorious, who chose your serenity for the bestowing of such benefactions, grant to you the fruits of the spirit and guide you to the University of the saints. Written at Oxford in our congregation in the twenty-fifth day of the month of January.

The most humble supplicant of your Serenity, the University of learning at Oxford.[1]

(2) TESTIMONIAL LETTER FOR MR. JOHN KING OF OXFORD

To all the children of Holy Church, our Mother, to whom this letter may come, the Chancellor of the University of Oxford and the whole assembly of masters ruling in the same send greeting in the arms of our Saviour. We believe that we present an offering in the sight of the highest truth, as often as we furnish a testimony of high praise to one excellent in virtue and in knowledge. Therefore we, — wishing all whom it may concern to know of the commendable life and the fragrance of honest conversation of our beloved brother, Master John King, M. A. and student in Sacred Theology, a prudent Procurator of our University who has filled his office most efficiently ; we therefore, as we have said, wishing all to know, as we are bound to do, — and to prevent so bright a light from being hid beneath the bushel of silence, — do bear witness by this letter that, through the commendable merits of our aforesaid brother and his study, he has attained such proficiency that the fragrant fame of his name — which the praise of his excellent action has exalted to the pinnacle of glory with us — could not be concealed : but from the height of its exalted pedestal it has furnished a living example to all scholars for emulation, and a great light to all people for profitable instruction. And so, while adorning our University with his presence and outshining all in the maturity and dignity of his character, he won the love of all by his spotless name. We commend him therefore to your worshipful reverences, earnestly praying that you will show yourselves favorable and kind to him, both out of regard for our

[1] *Epistolae Academicae Oxon.*, I, p. 177.

University and for his deserts.   In witness of which, and that all may know more fully about his laudable character, we have caused this letter to be sealed for said Master John with the seal of our University.

Given at Oxford in the Congregation-house, February 9th, 1434.[1]

1 *Epistolae Academicae Oxon.*, I, p. 113.

BIBLIOGRAPHICAL NOTE

1. Additional Readings from the Sources.

MUNRO, D. C. *The Mediaeval Student.* (Translations and Reprints from the Original Sources of European History, Vol. II, No. 3.) The student should not fail to procure this little pamphlet, which is a necessary supplement to several of the readings in the present collection. It contains useful explanatory notes as well as important documents. Price, ten cents. Longmans, Green & Co., New York City.

ROBINSON, J. H. *Readings in European History.* Vol. I, chap. xix, and especially pp. 446–461. Readings on Abelard, Aristotle in the Universities, Roger Bacon.

HENDERSON, E. F. *Select Historical Documents of the Middle Ages,* pp. 262–266. Charter of the University of Heidelberg, 1386.

2. General References on the History of Mediaeval Universities.

RASHDALL, HASTINGS. *The Universities of Europe in the Middle Ages.* Oxford: The Clarendon Press, 1895. 1273 pages, 2 vols. in three parts. Much the best work on the subject; based on the sources. Indispensable for reference.

MULLINGER, J. B. *Encyclopedia Britannica,* Art. *Universities.* "The first tolerably correct (though very brief) account which has appeared in English." Includes university history to 1882.

Encyclopedia Britannica and other encyclopedias. The student who may not have access to works mentioned in this list is reminded that brief accounts of the men and the subjects here considered are often to be found in good encyclopedias.

3. Bibliographies.

The best single collection of references to the extensive literature of the subject is in Rashdall's work, though this does not include books and articles published since 1895. Compayré (see below) includes a brief list. References to sources and secondary works on the Seven Liberal Arts are published by Abelson; references relating to university text-books of Greek origin by Loomis (see below).

4. Text-books.

COMPAYRÉ, G. *Abelard and the Origin and Early History of Universities*. New York: Charles Scribner's Sons, 1892. Still the best single text-book for class use. Contains numerous errors, which should be corrected by comparison with Rashdall.

WOODWARD, W. H., *editor*. *Mediaeval Schools and Universities*. Cambridge Contributions to Modern History, I. New York: G. P. Putnam's Sons. This work, which is still in preparation, will probably supersede Compayré.

5. References to Special Topics.

All of the topics treated in this collection of readings are discussed by Rashdall and Compayré. Page references may be found by use of the indexes appended to their books.

Introduction. On the historical point of view see J. H. ROBINSON, *Readings in European History*, Vol. I, Chap. I; on the place and use of documents, and other questions relating to the study of history, LANGLOIS and SEIGNOBOS, *Introduction to the Study of History*.

Abelard. MCCABE, JOSEPH. *Abelard.* A scholarly study, in brilliant style. Chaps. I–IV deal with Abelard as a teacher. The best biography in English.

John of Salisbury. POOLE, R. L. *Illustrations of the History of Mediaeval Thought*, passim. National Dictionary of Biography, Art. *John of Salisbury*.

University Studies. ABELSON, PAUL. *The Seven Liberal Arts.* The best study in English. Contains much information regarding university text-books in these subjects. LOOMIS, LOUISE R. *Mediaeval Hellenism.* Valuable information concerning the history and the translations of the works of Aristotle, Galen, Hippocrates, and other Greek writers. ZELLER, E. *Aristotle and the Earlier Peripatetics.* The standard treatise on the works of Aristotle, and their history.

The student is earnestly advised to spend a few hours in examining such copies of the mediaeval text-books as he may find in his college library. The time thus spent will do far more to clarify his ideas as to their character and extent than much talk about them. Old editions, often with the commentaries, may be available; some libraries possess MS. copies. Translations of the more important works of Aristotle may be found by reference to the library catalogue; among these may be mentioned the *Rhetoric,* by J. E. C. Welldon; the *Politics,* by B. Jowett; the *Ethics* (Nicomachean), by F. H. Peters; the *Poetics,* by S. H. Butcher. Of the *Corpus Juris Civilis,* the *Institutes* have been translated by T. C. Sandars; the first part of the *Digest* by C. H. Monro. The *Corpus Juris Canonici* as it was known in the middle ages has not been translated. This is true also of most books on the Seven Liberal Arts. Some works of Galen and Hippocrates have been done into English; but these translations are old, and probably inaccurate.

Academic Letters. HASKINS, C. H. *The Life of Mediaeval Students as Illustrated by their Letters.* American Historical Review, 1897–1898. A brief but important study, from the sources; refers to several of the letters here printed.